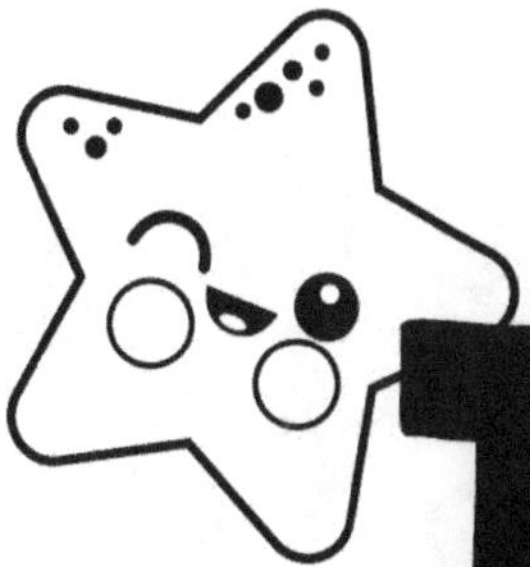

This book belongs to

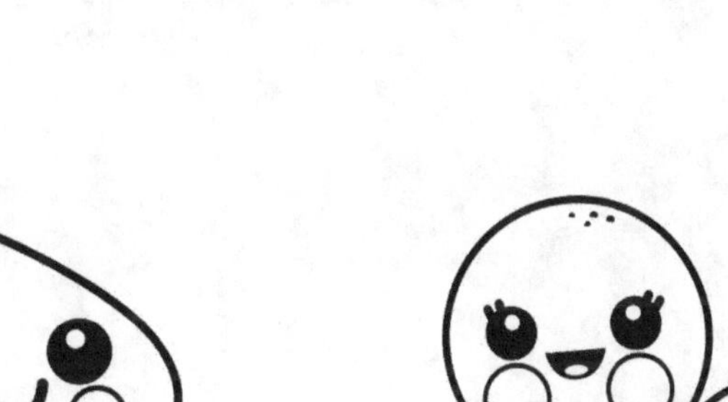

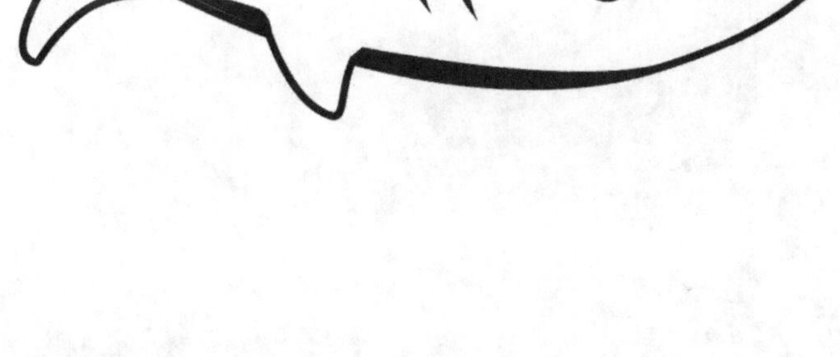

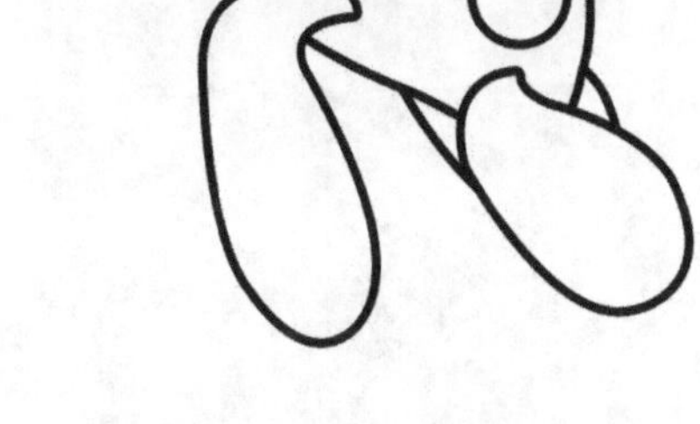

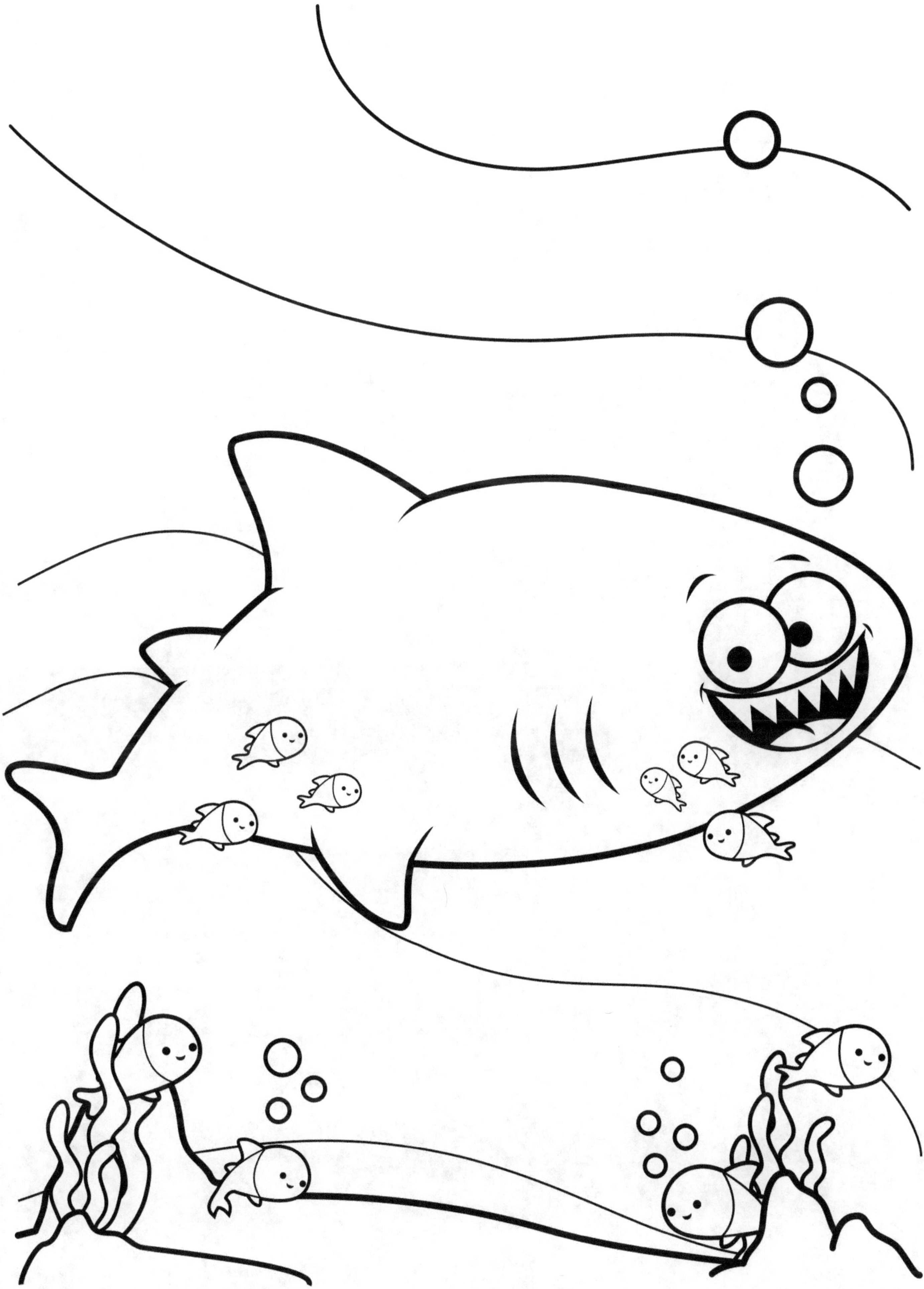

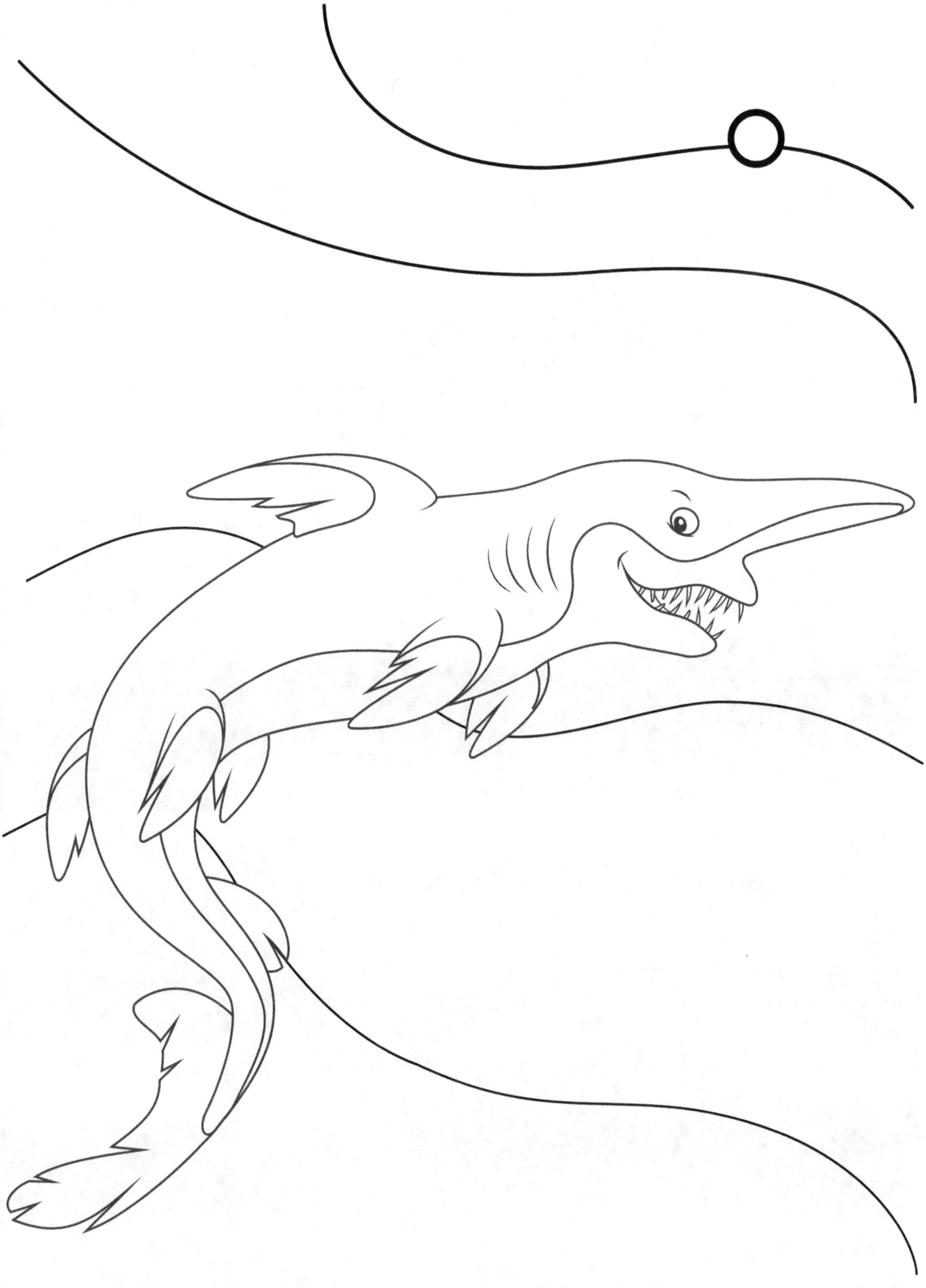

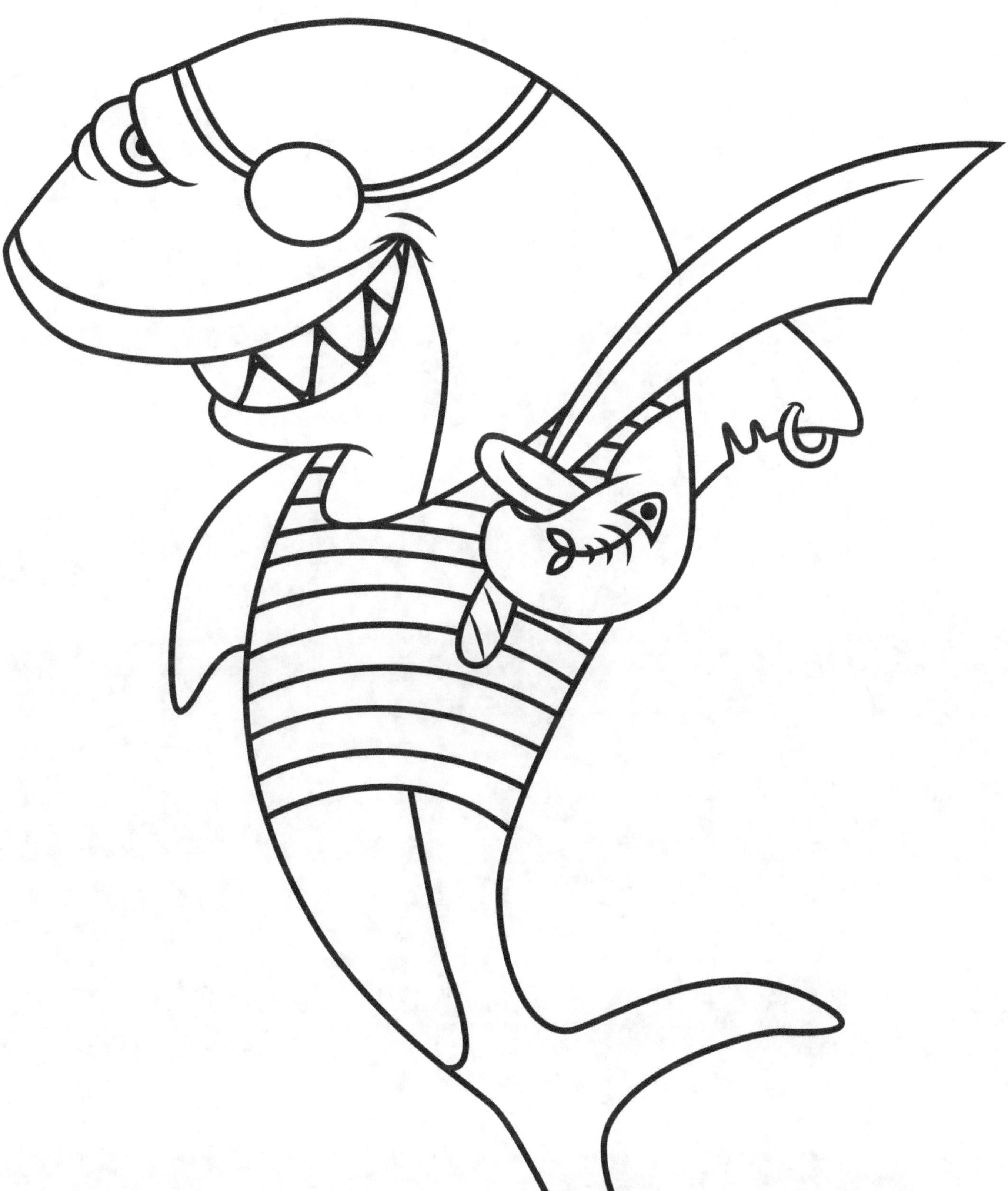

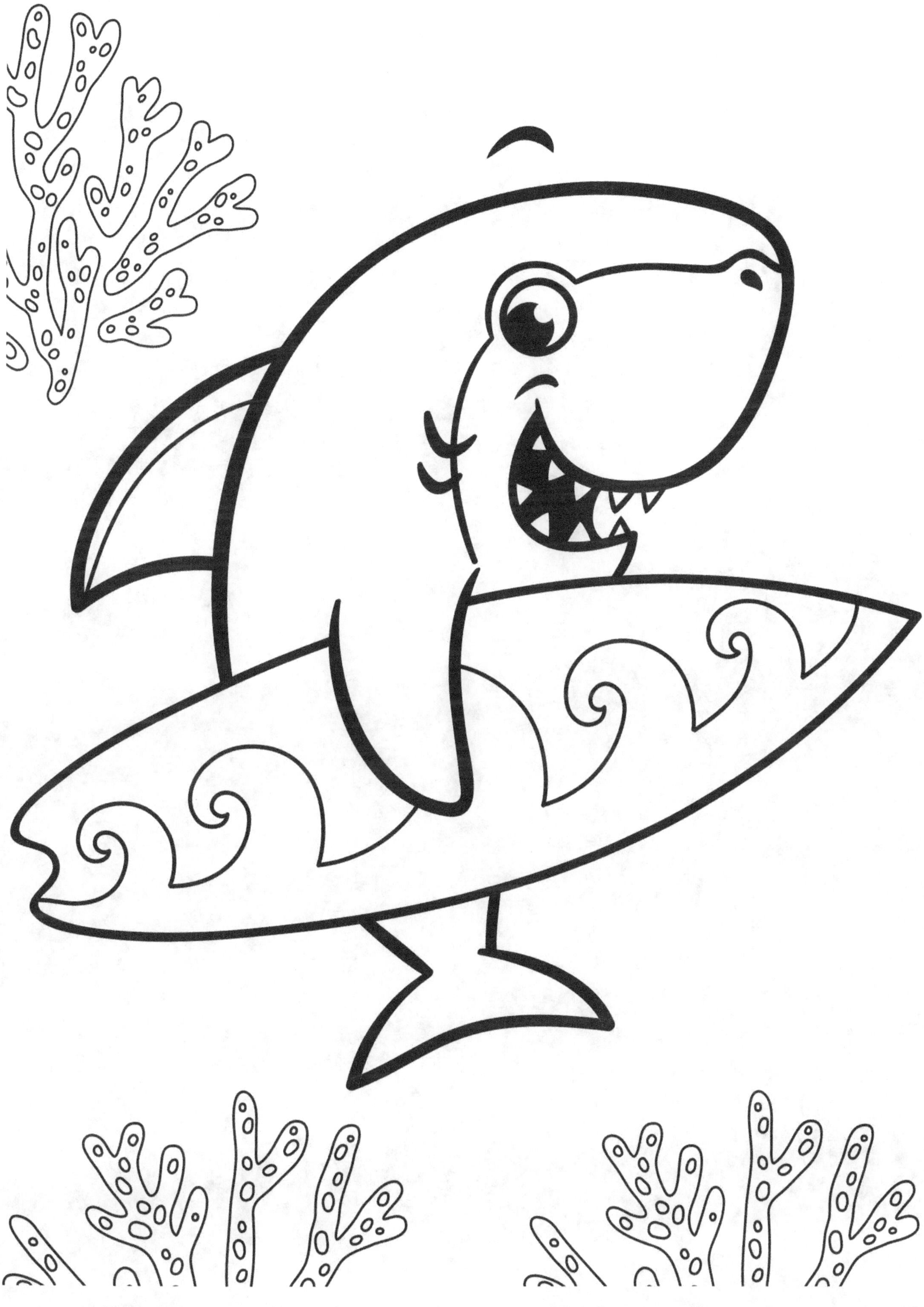

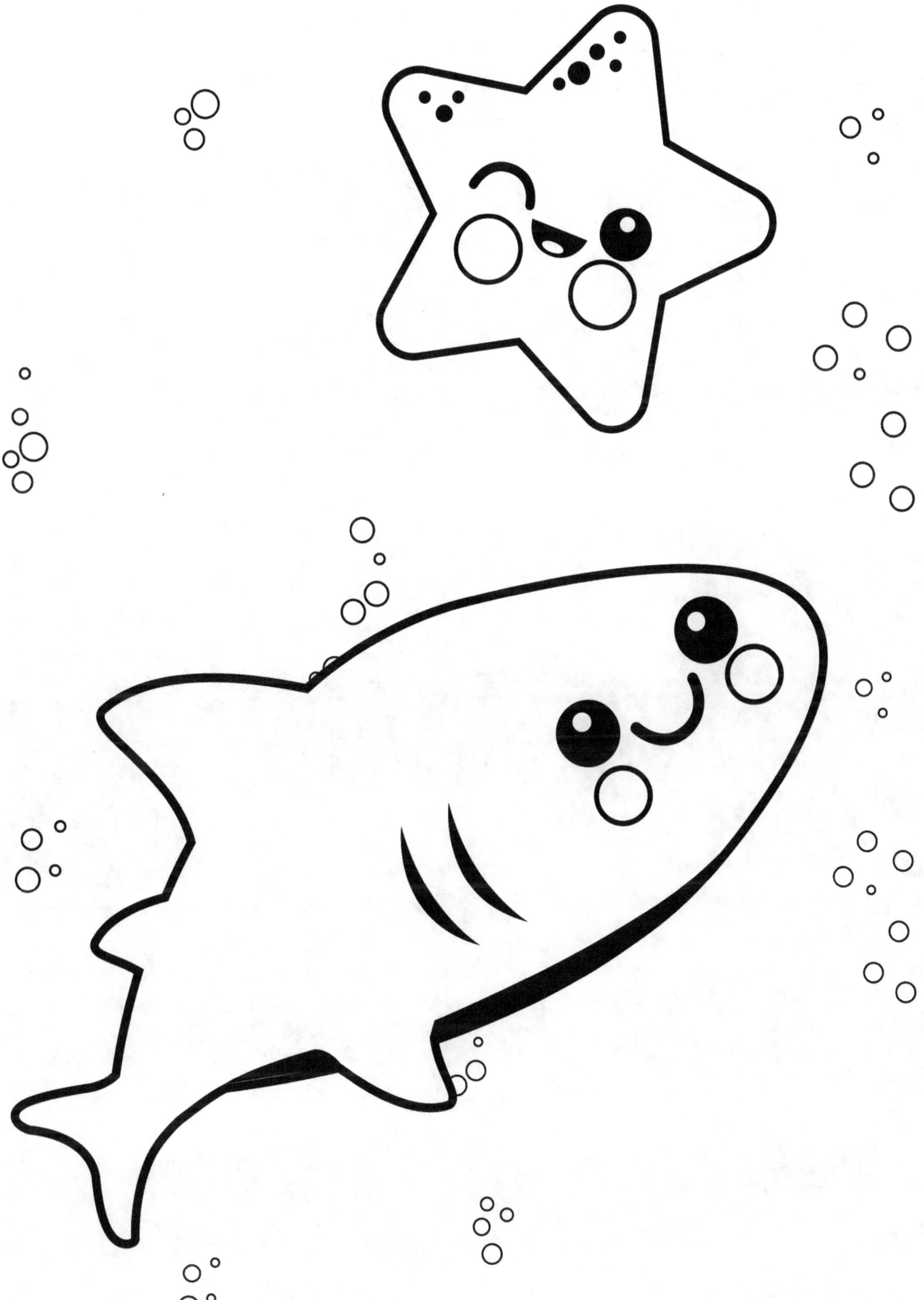

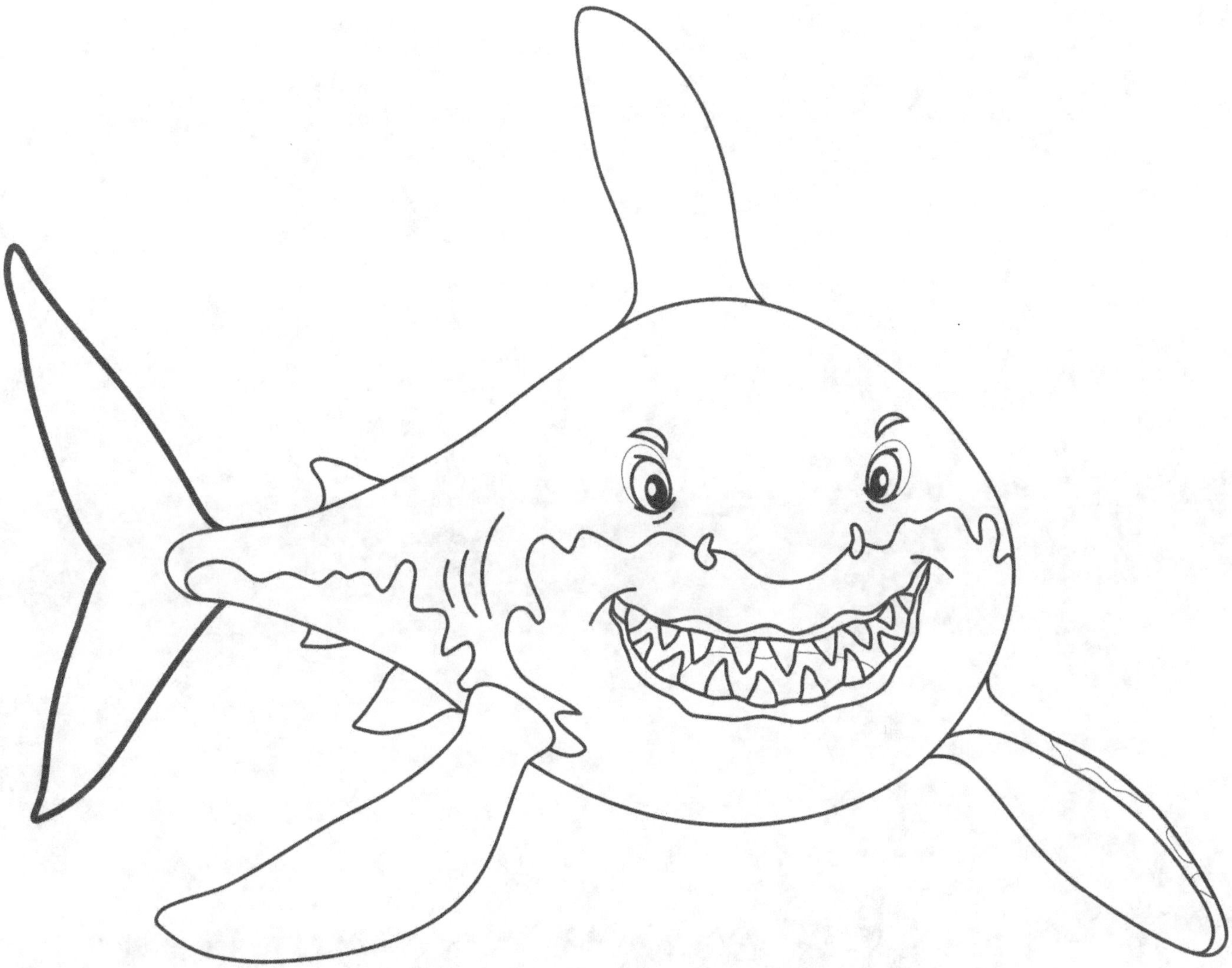

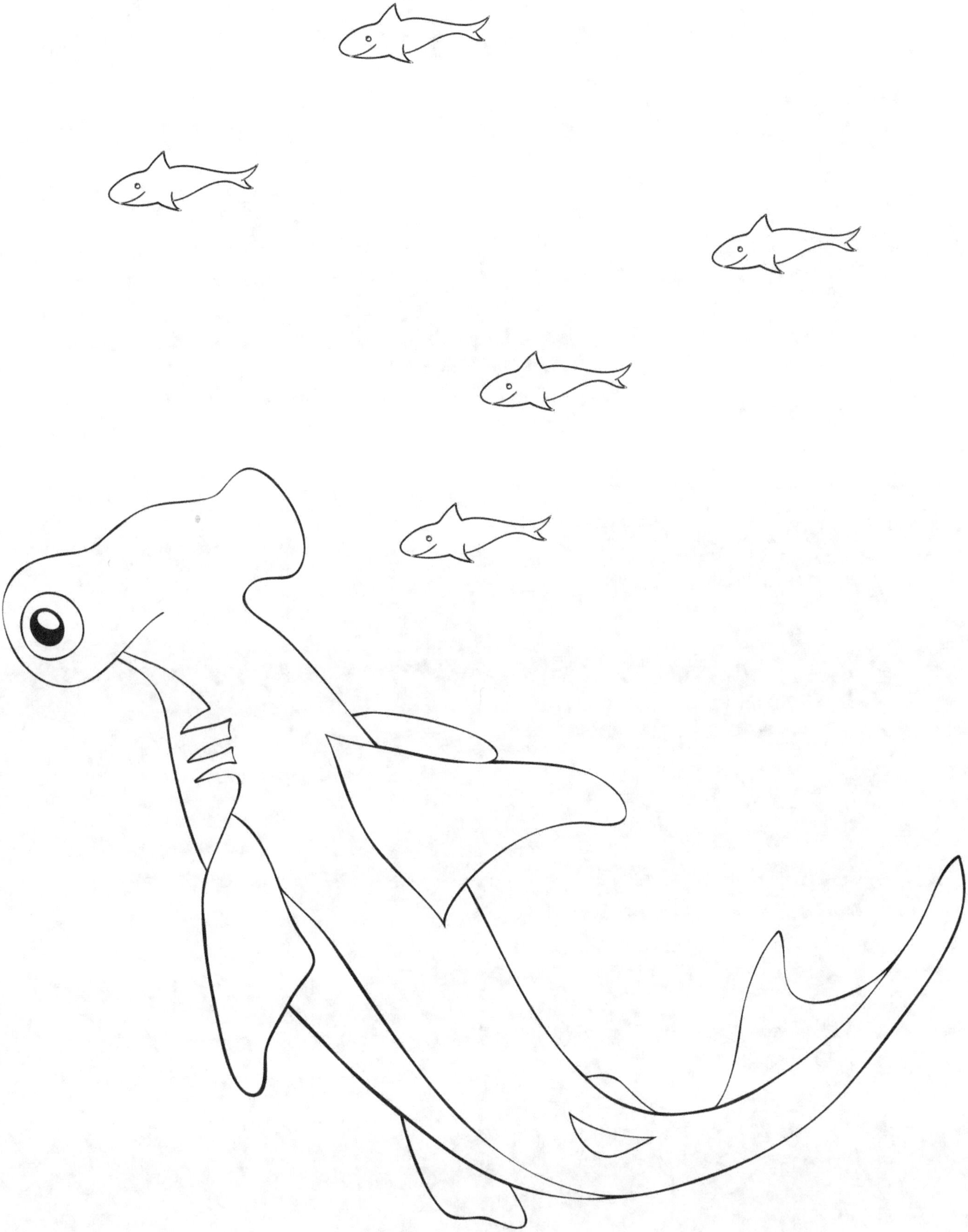

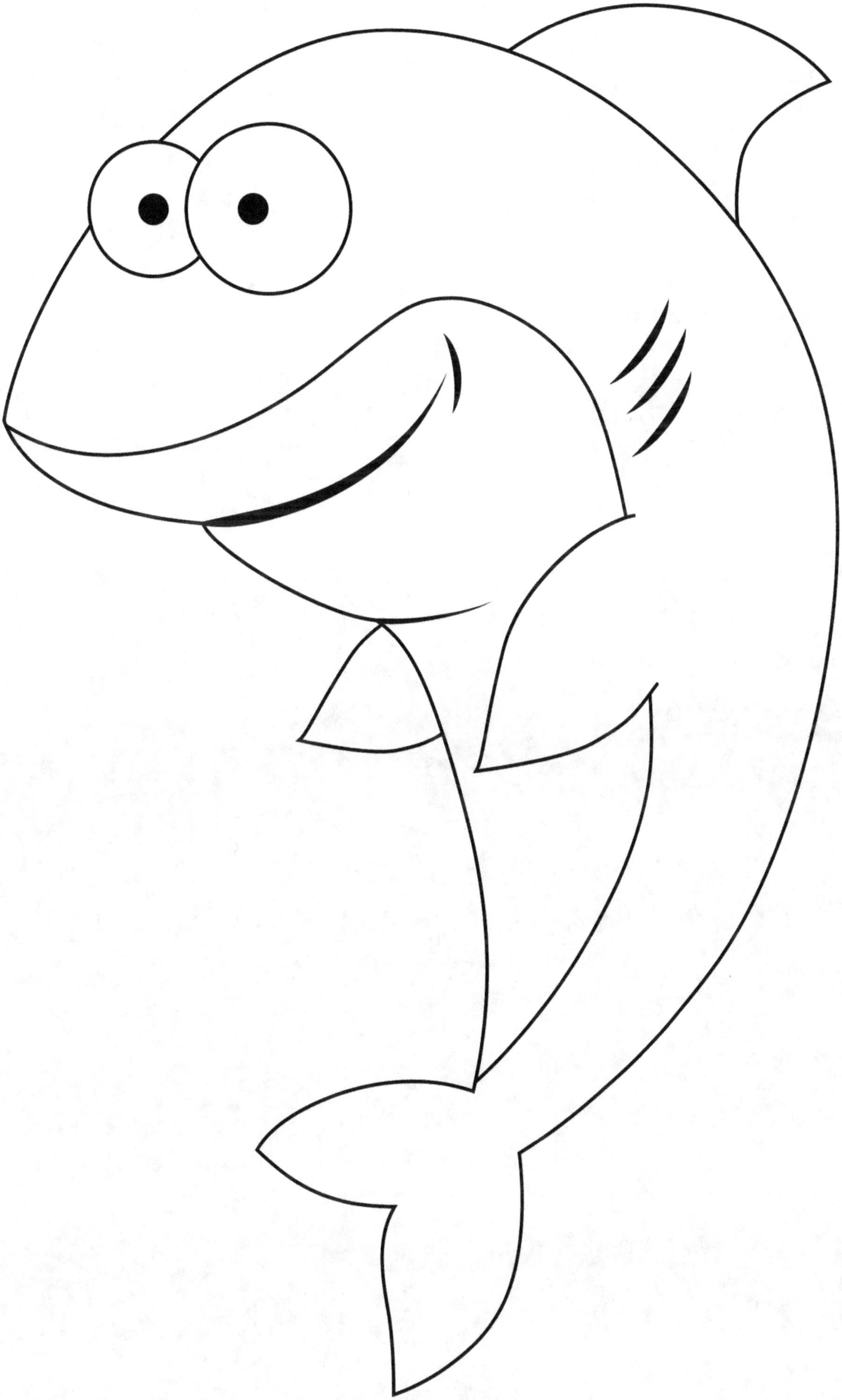

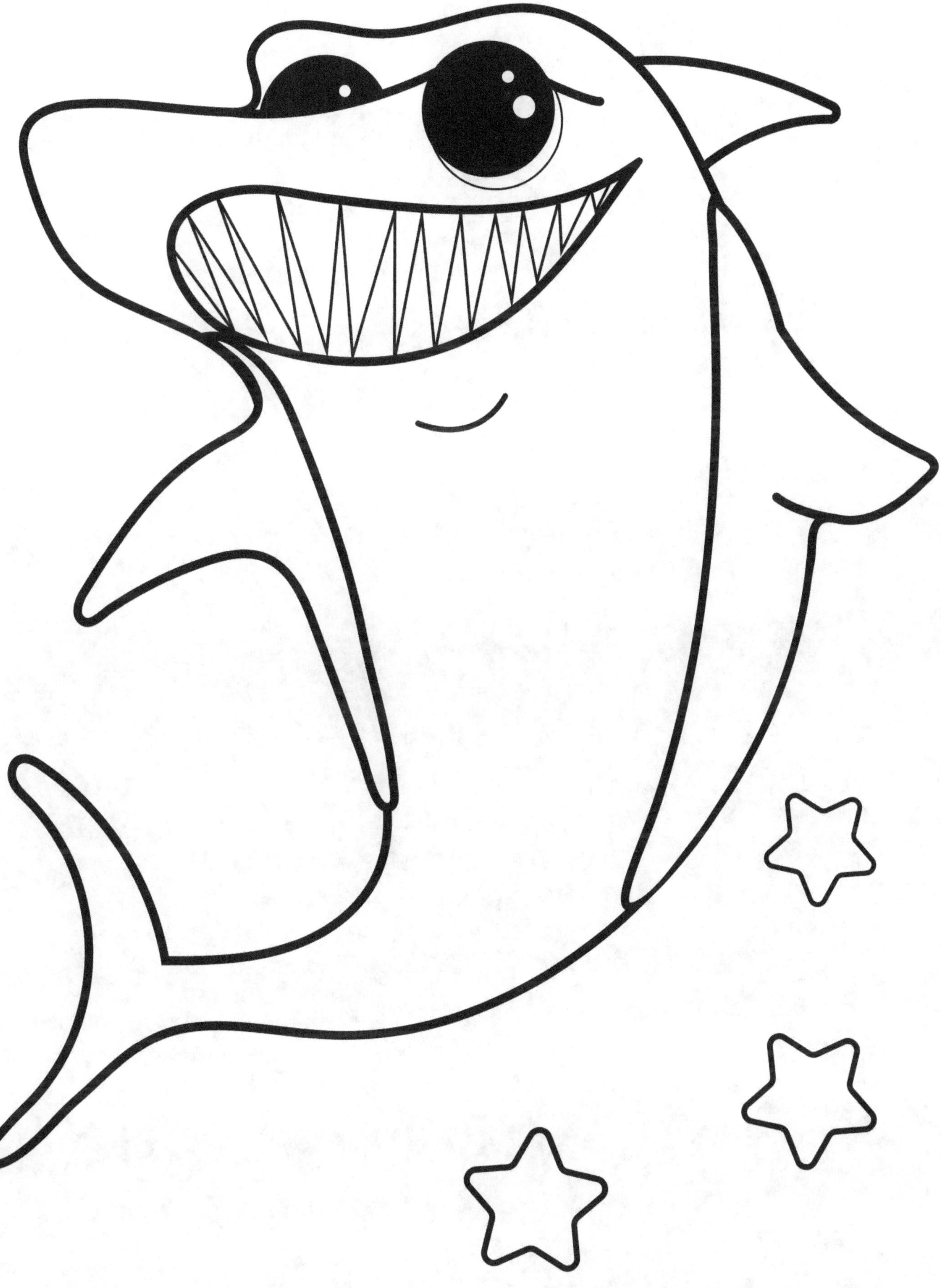

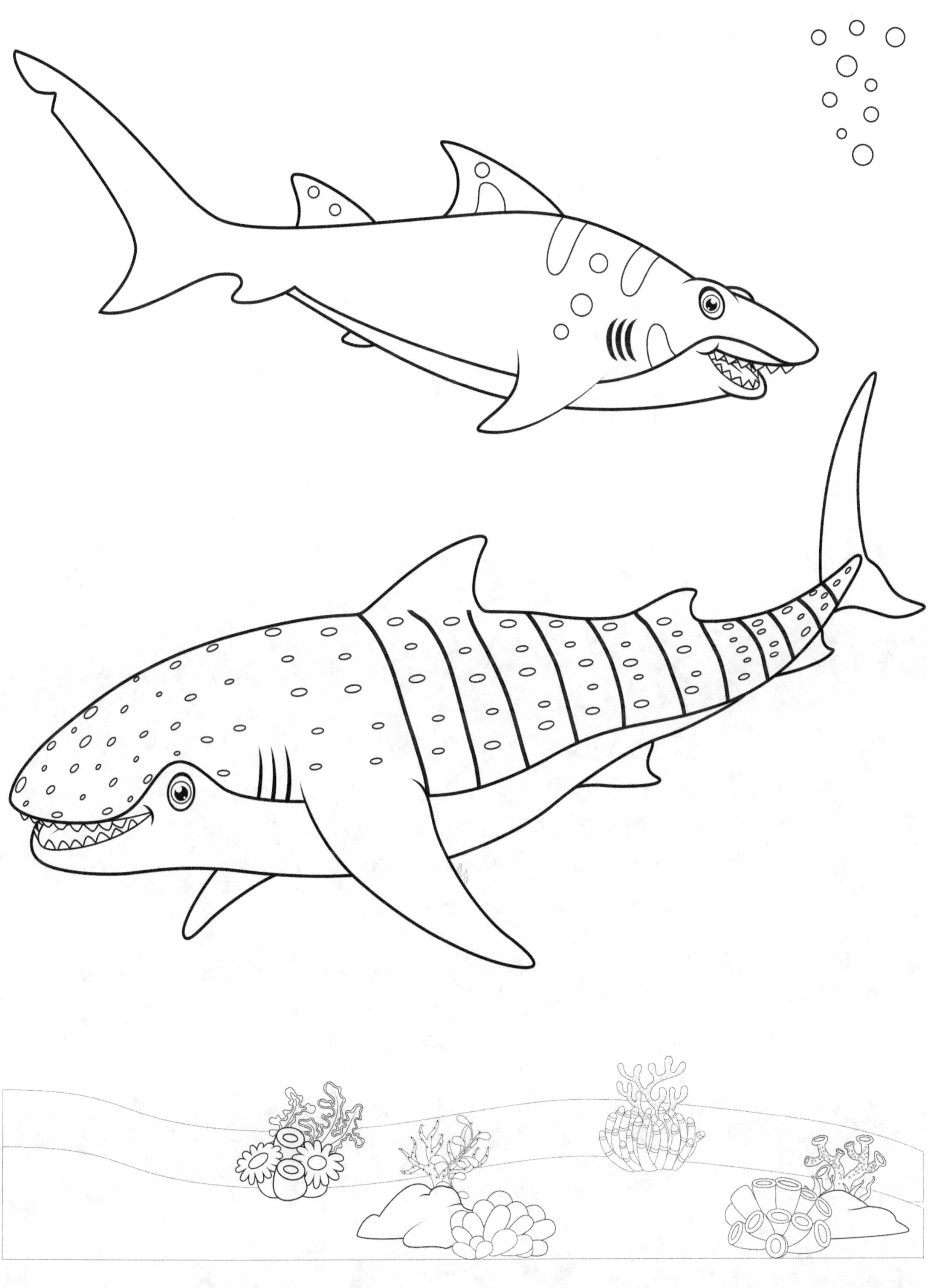

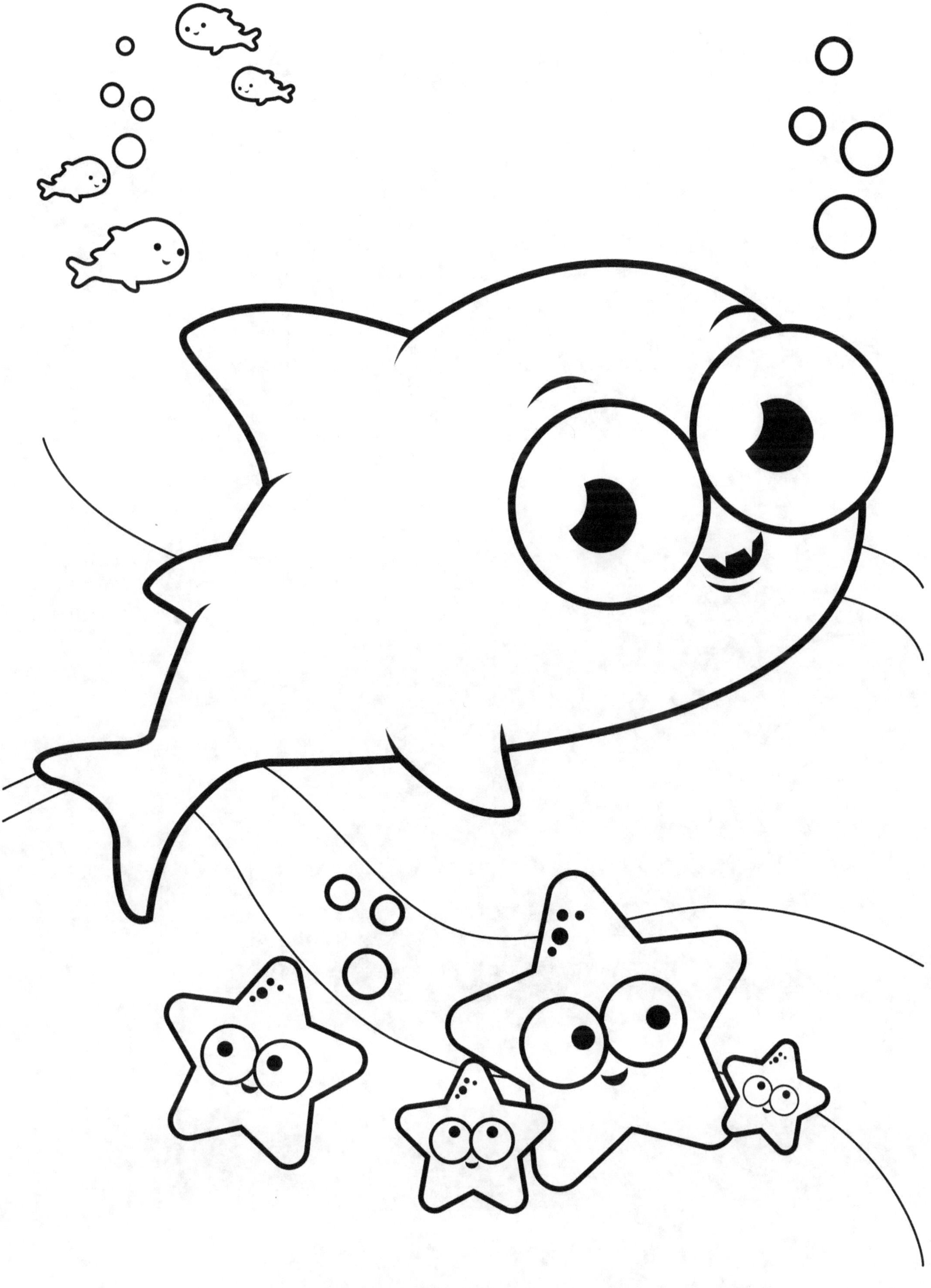

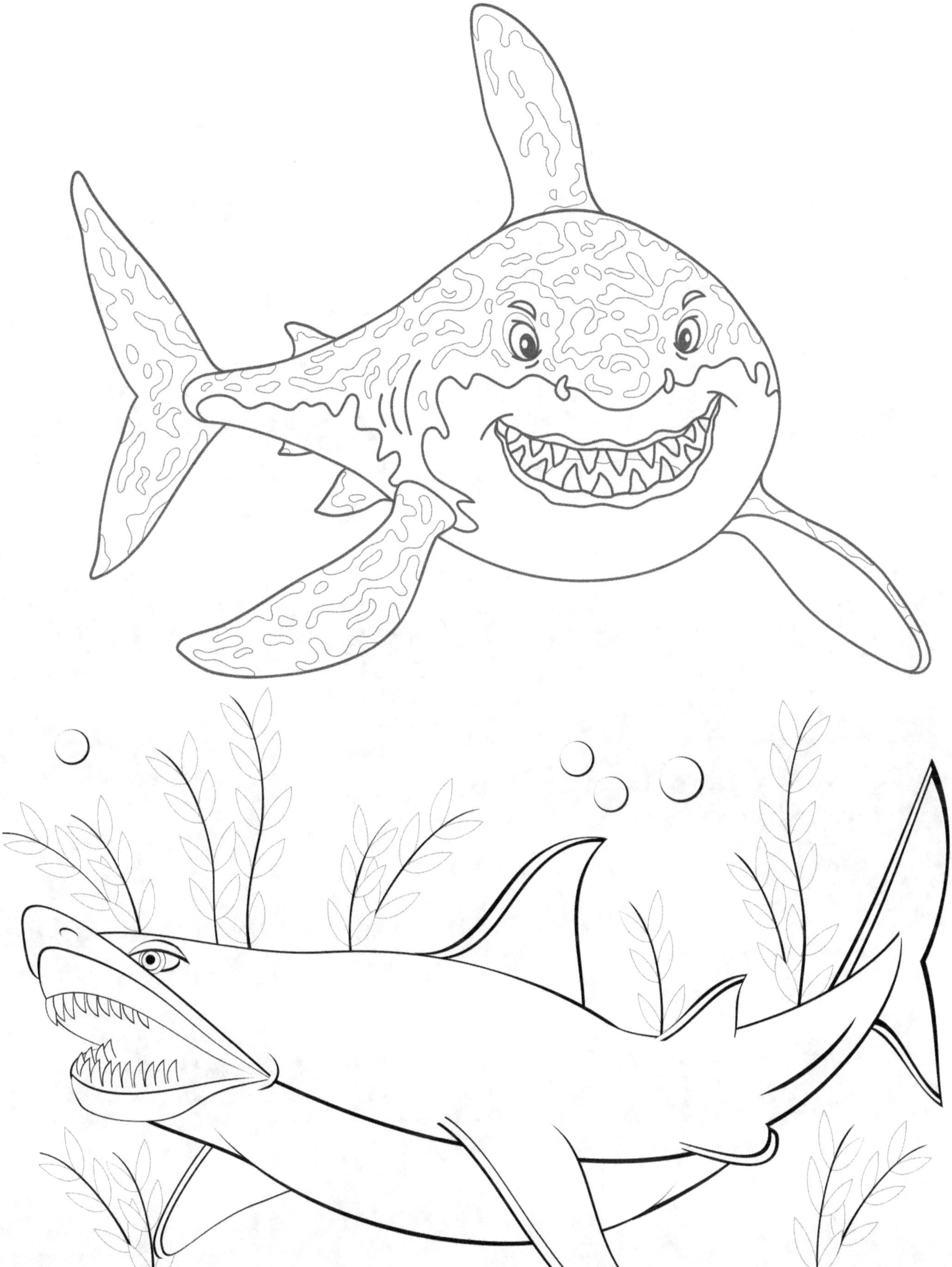

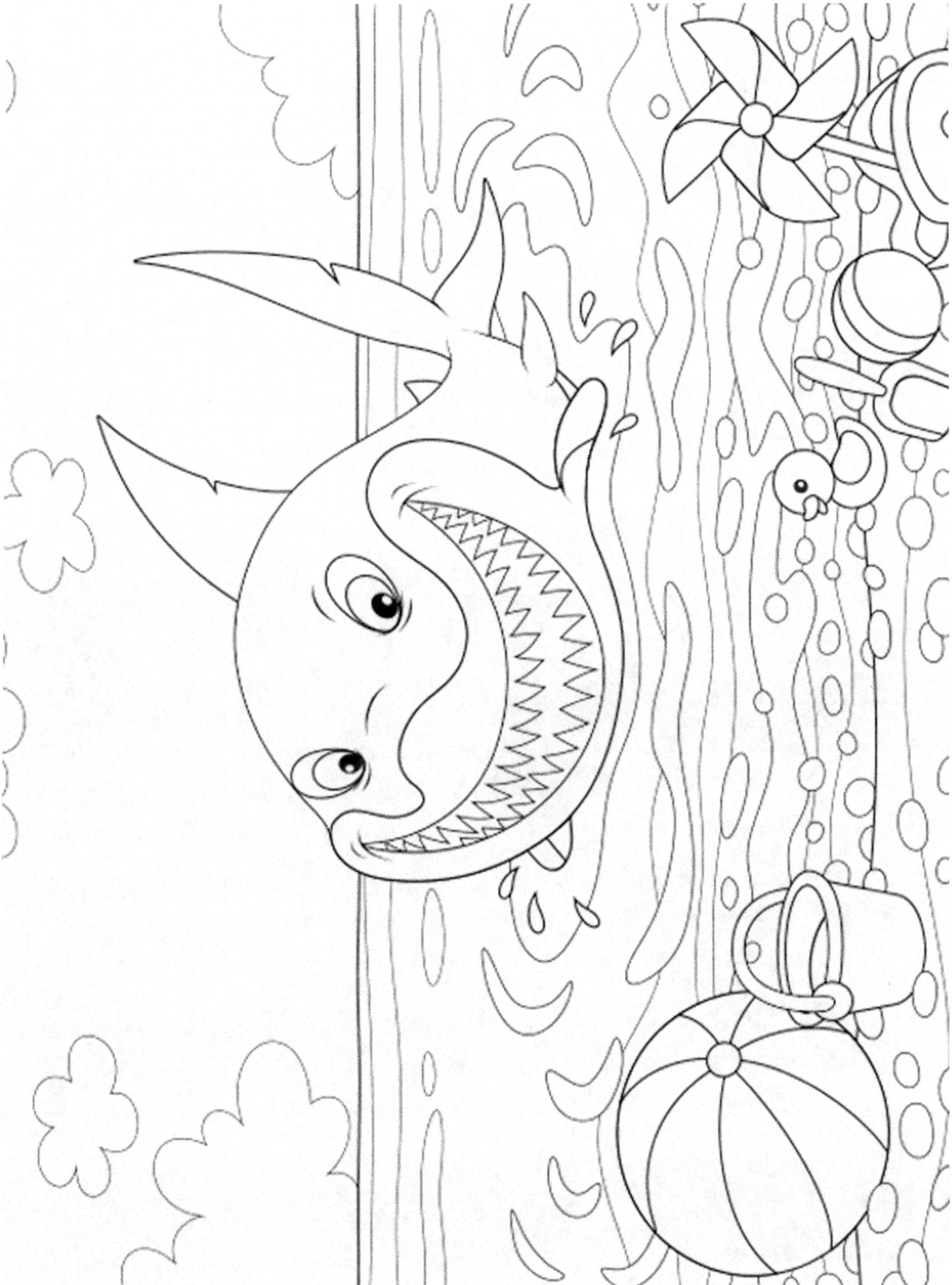

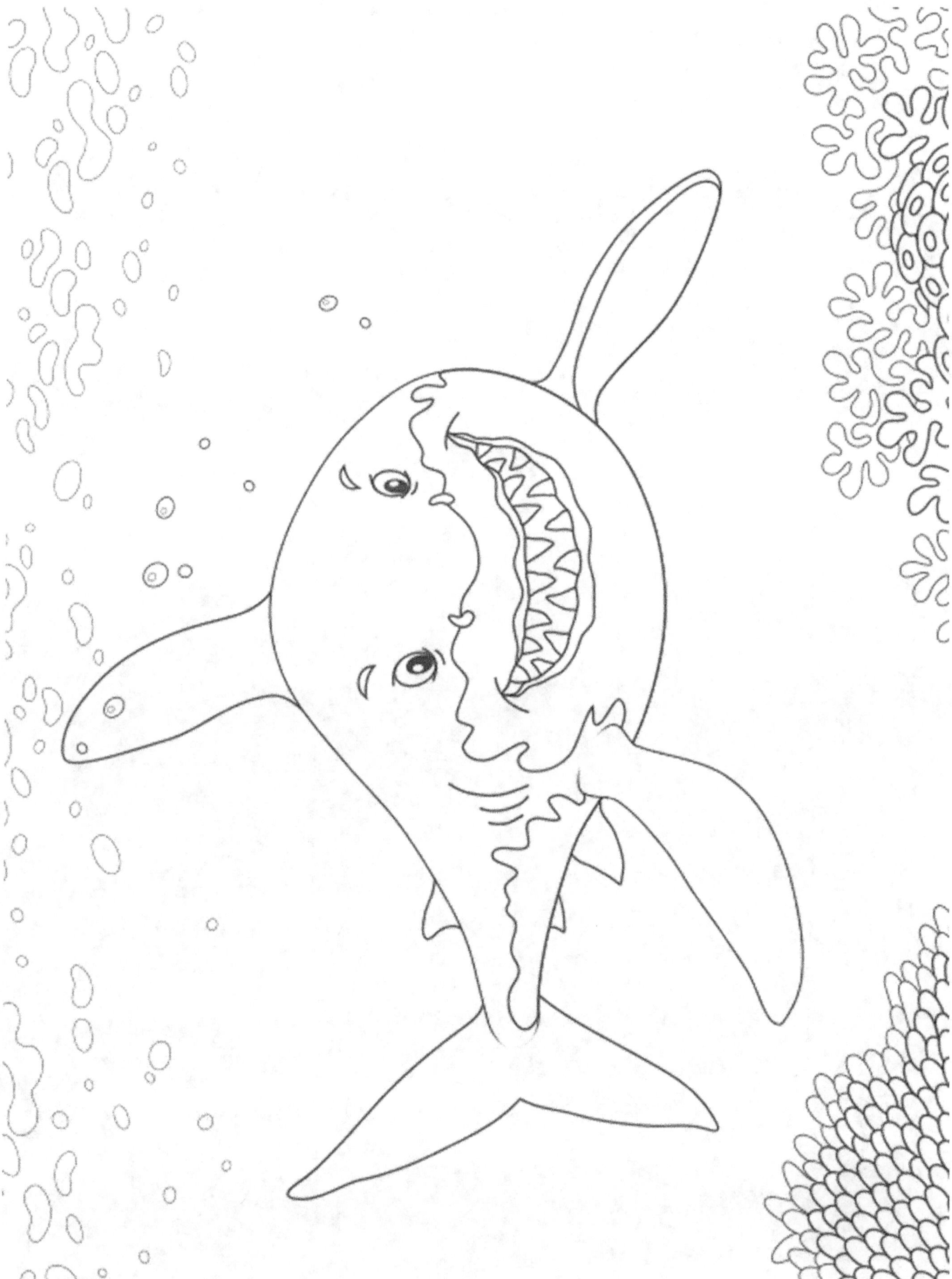

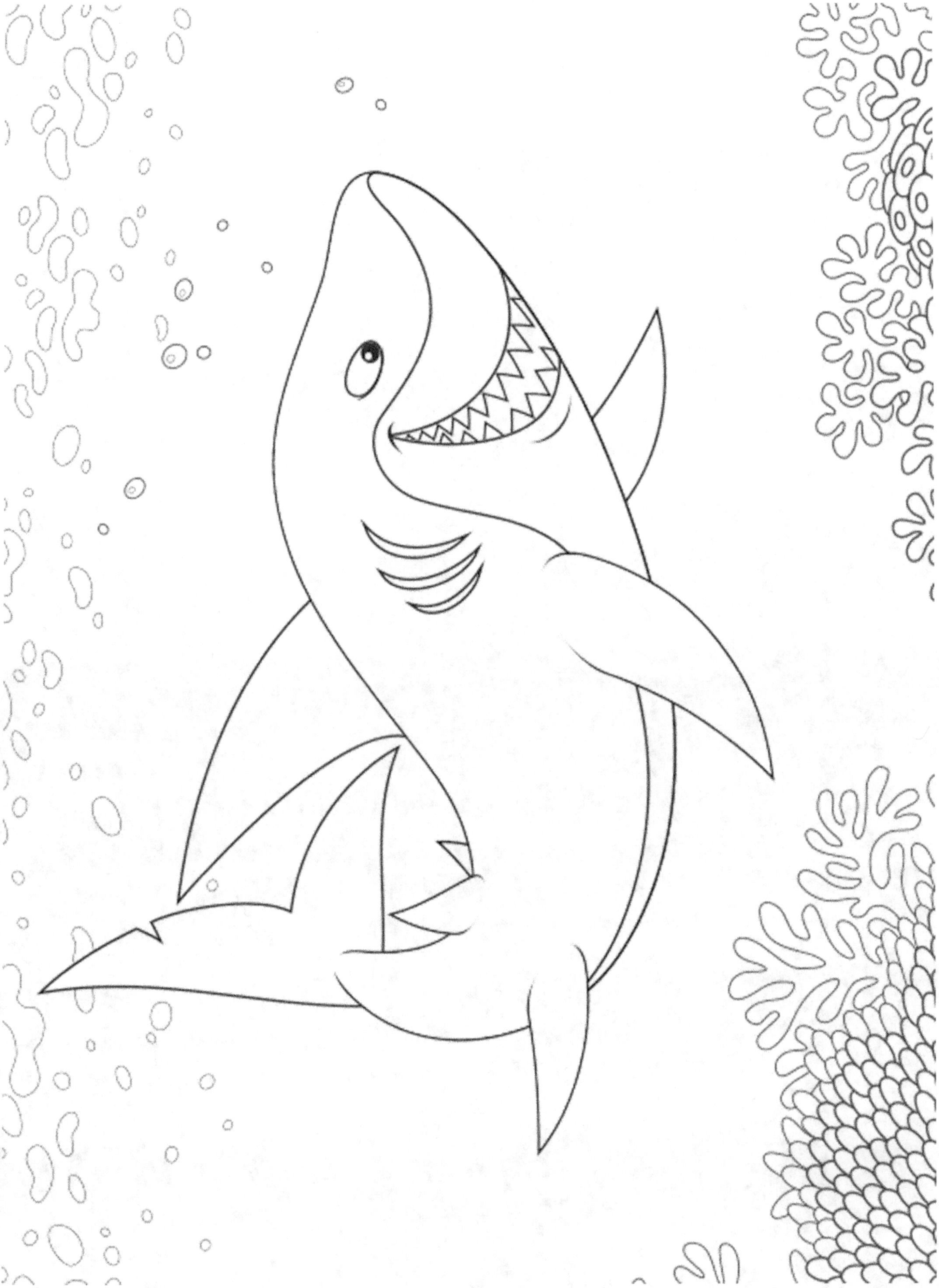

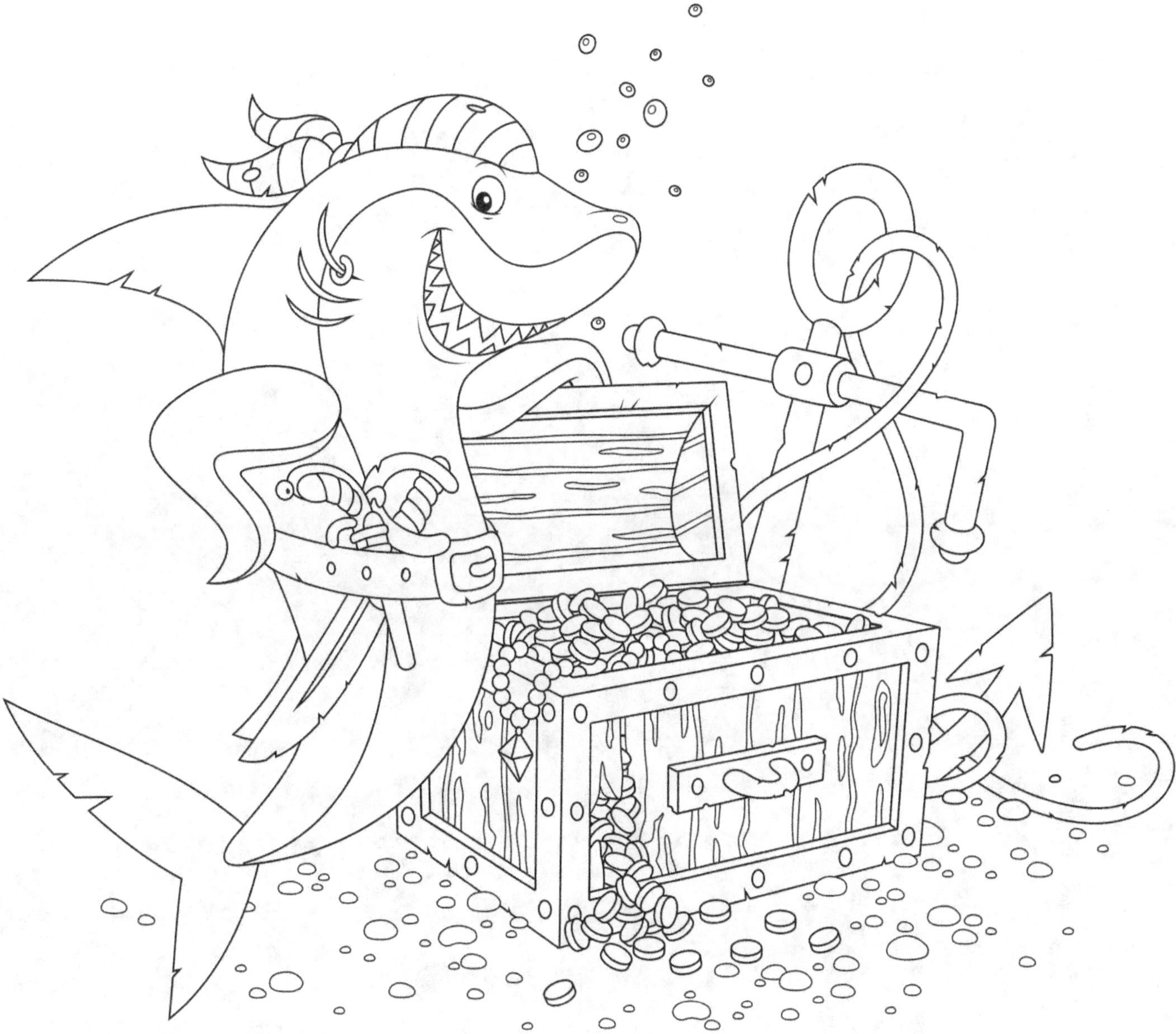

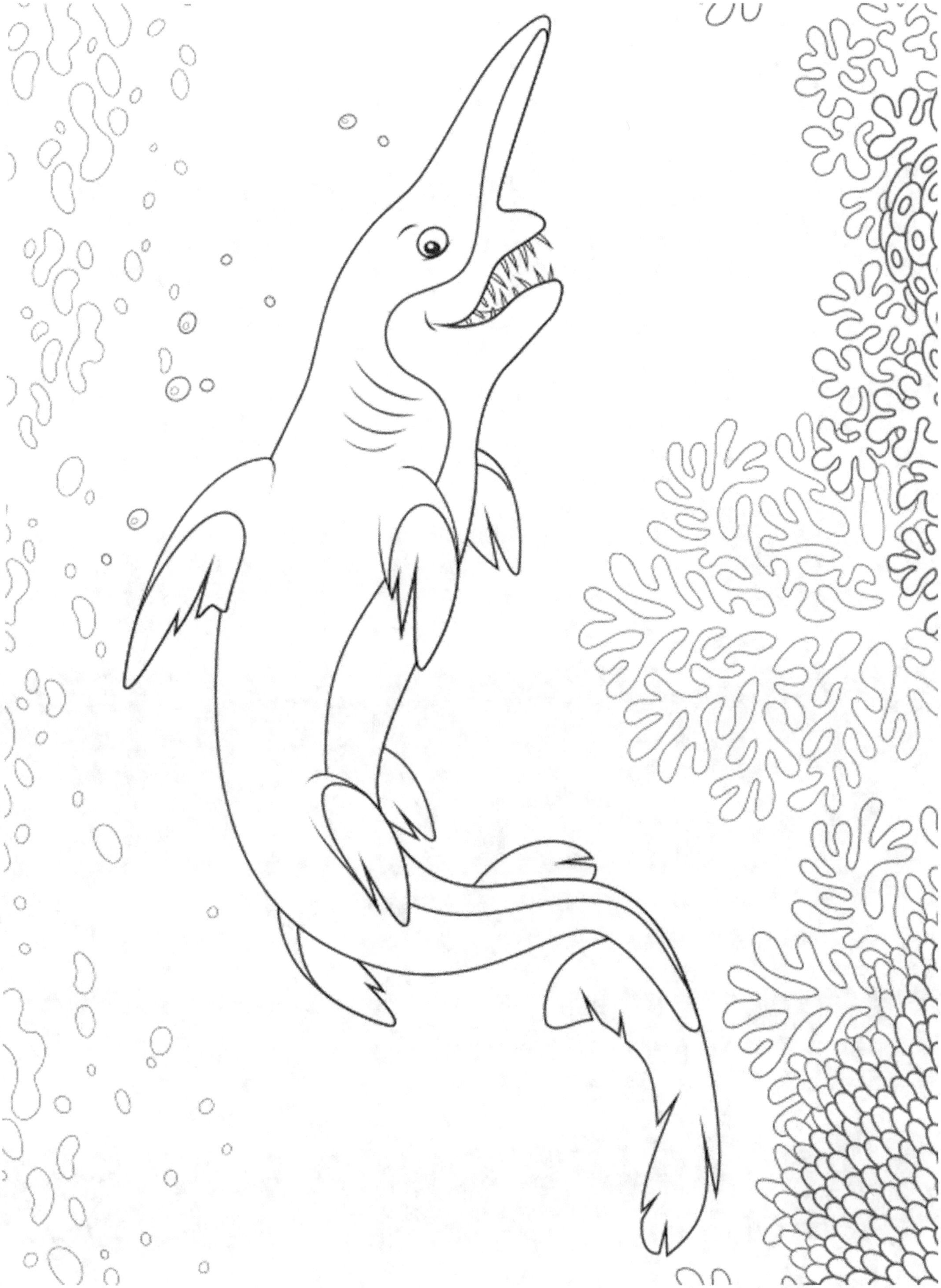

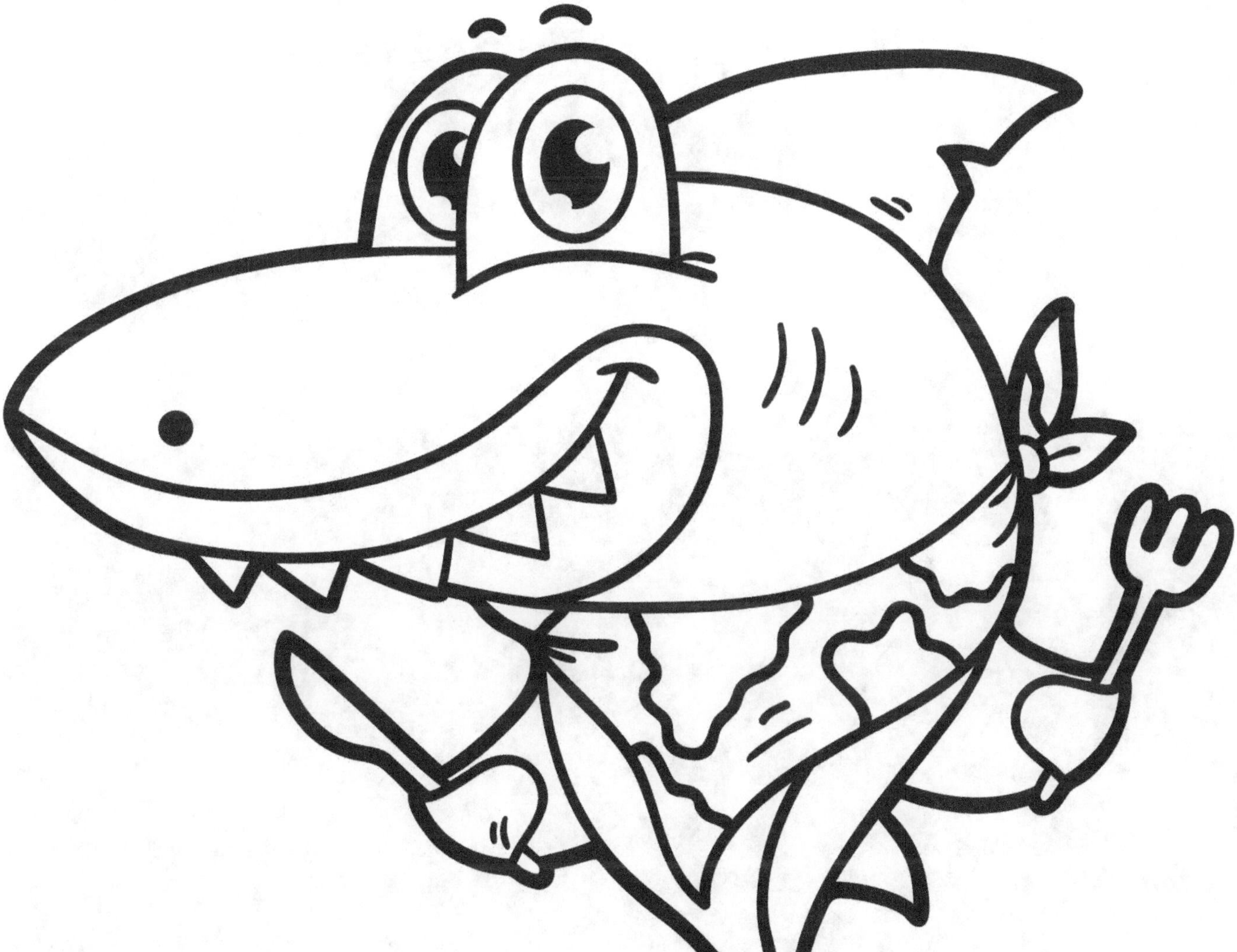

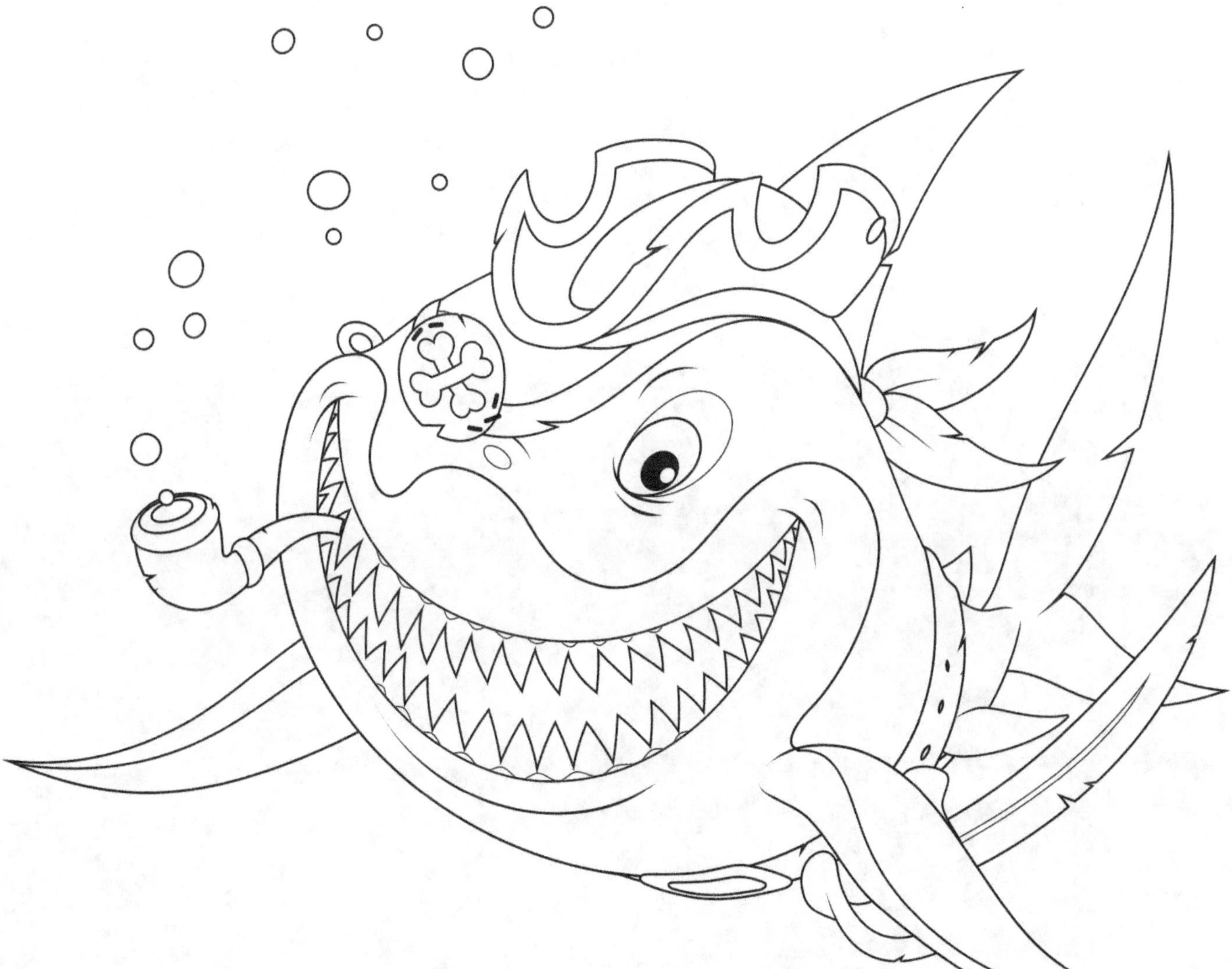

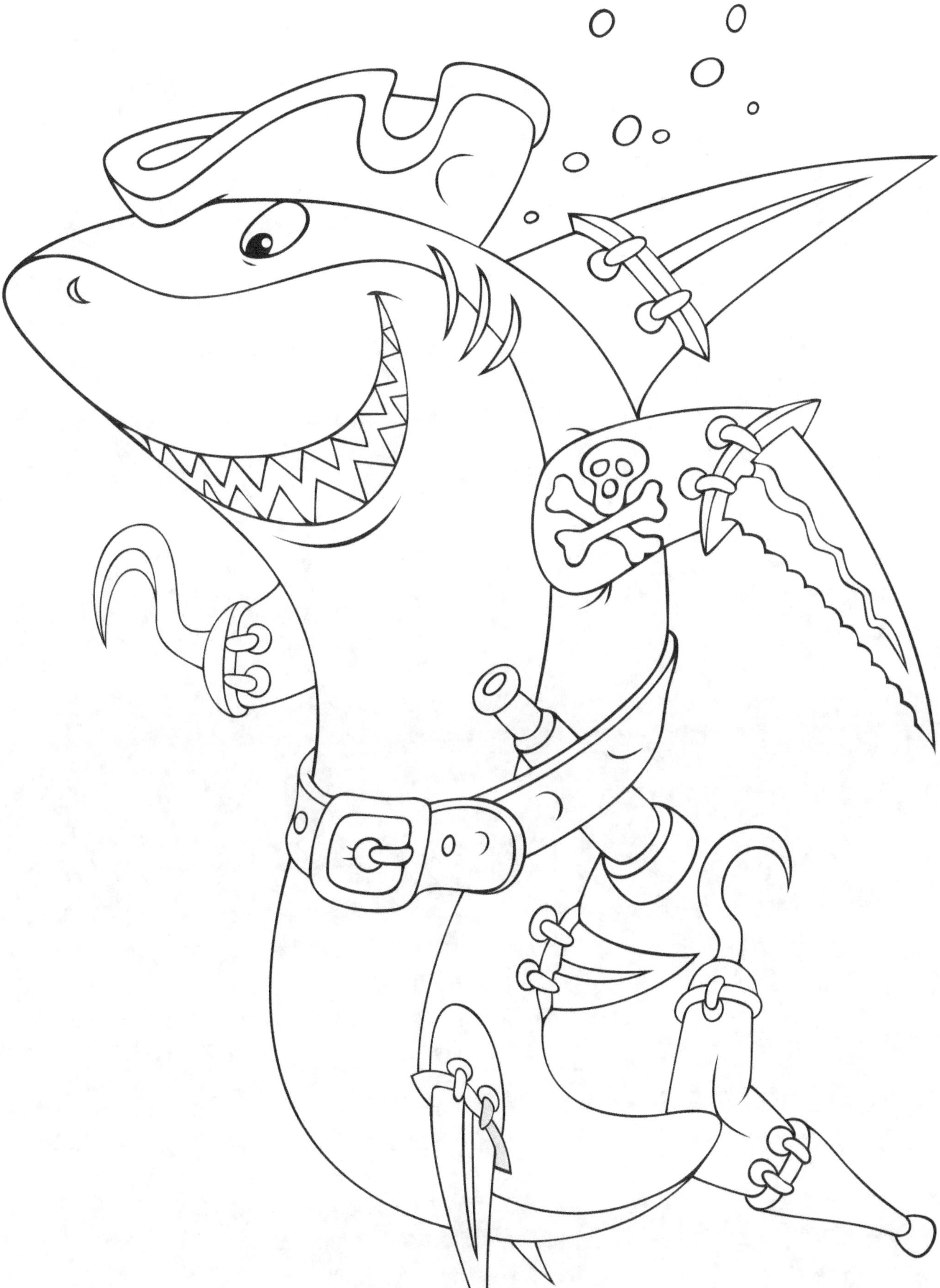

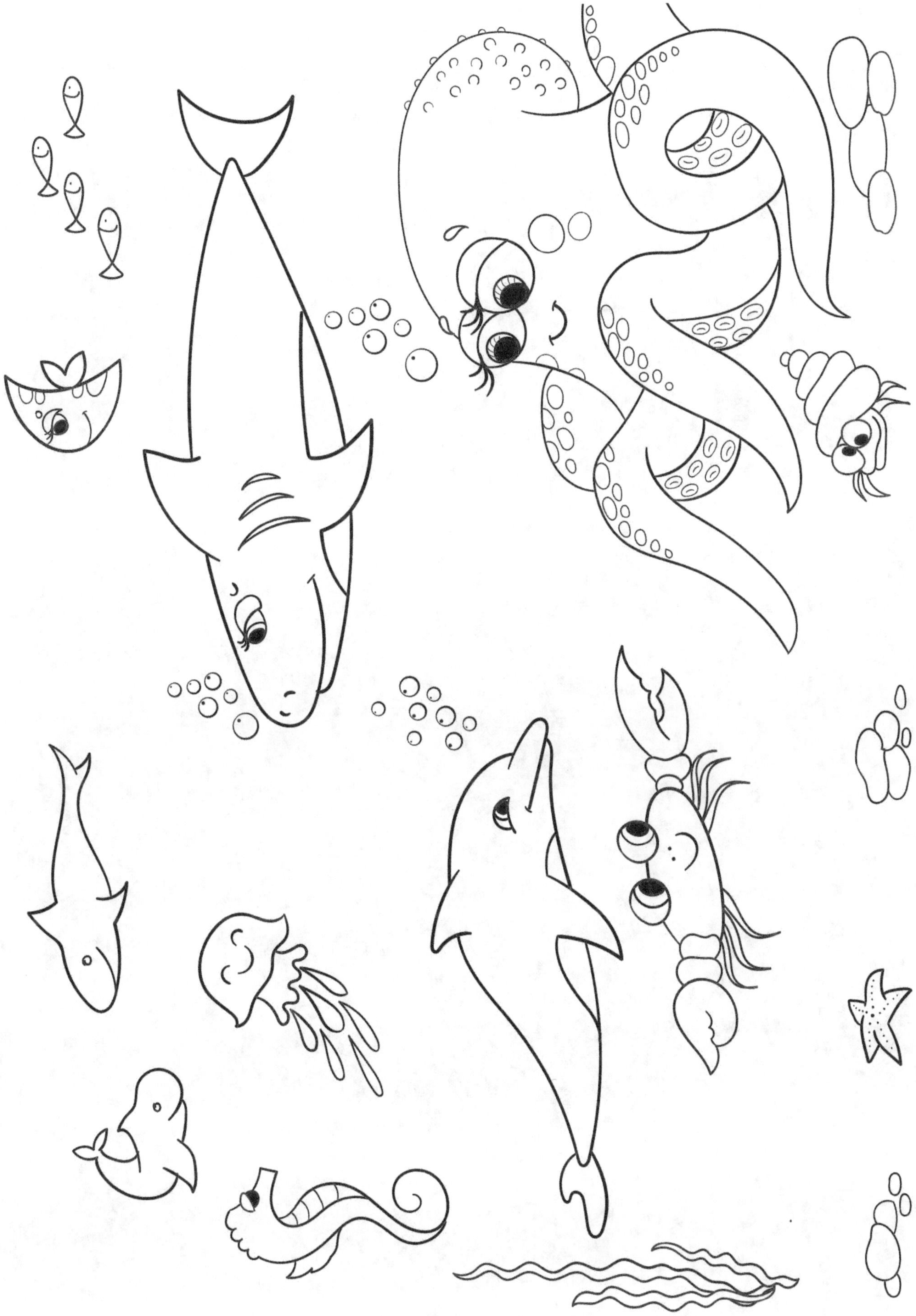

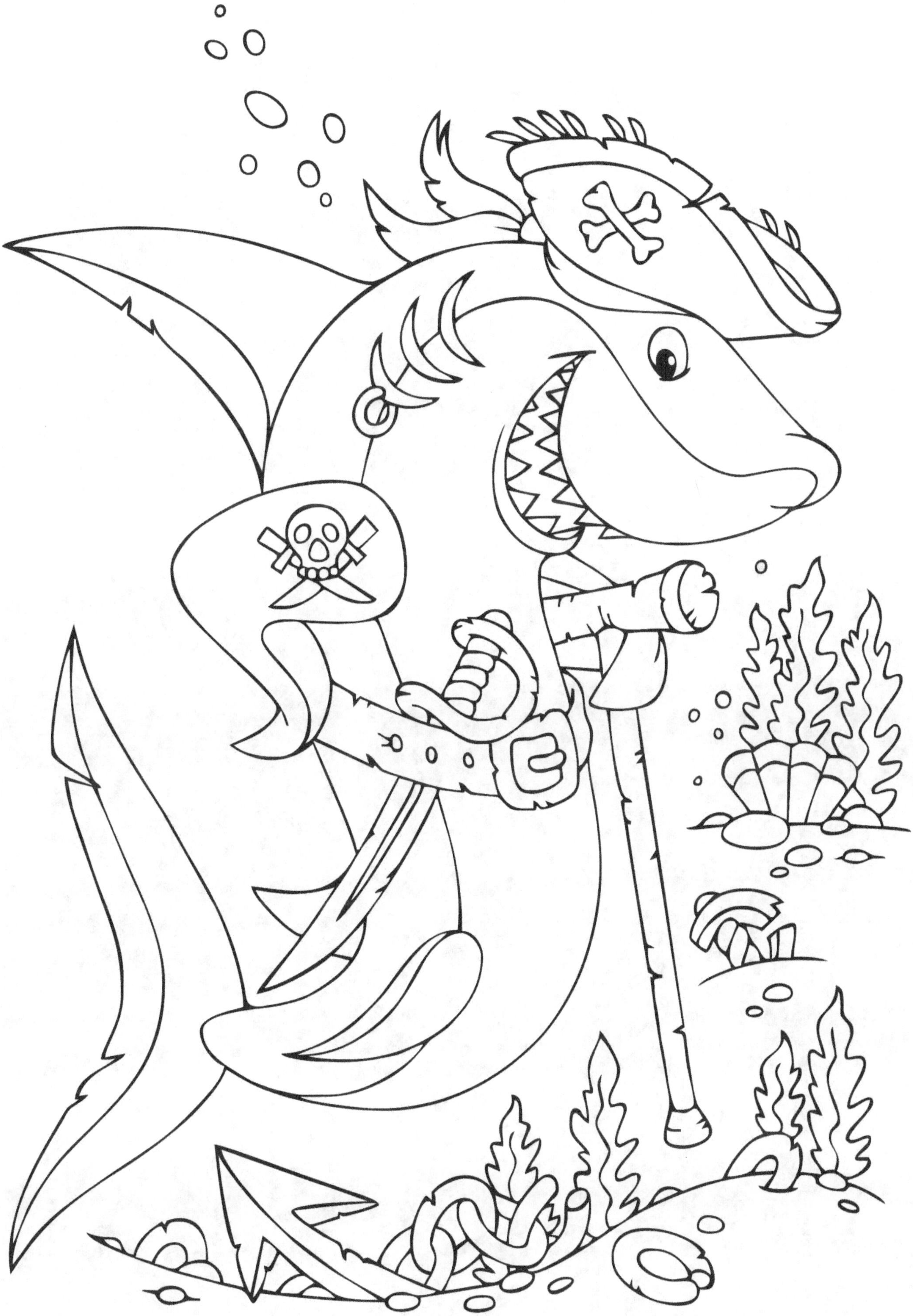

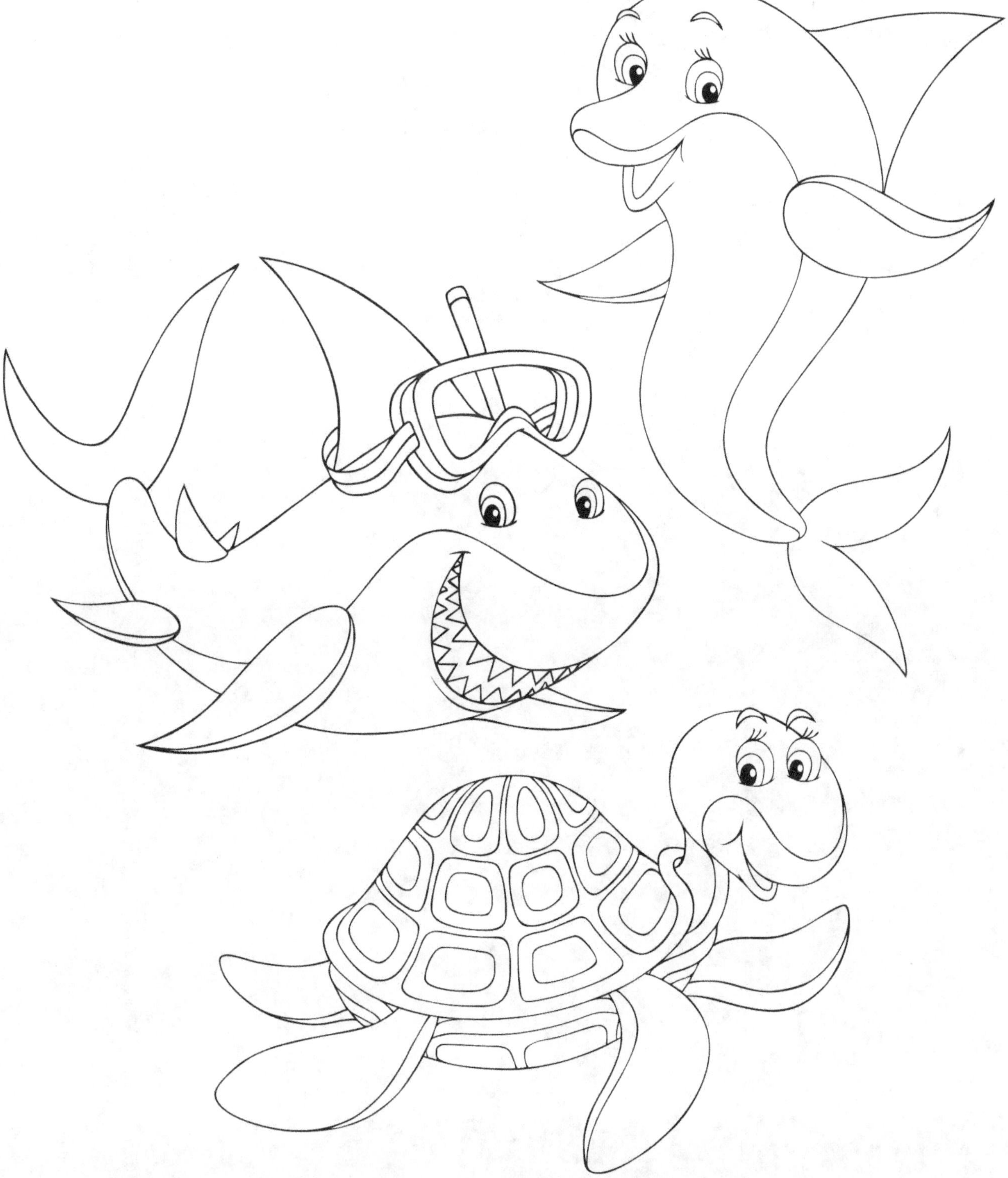

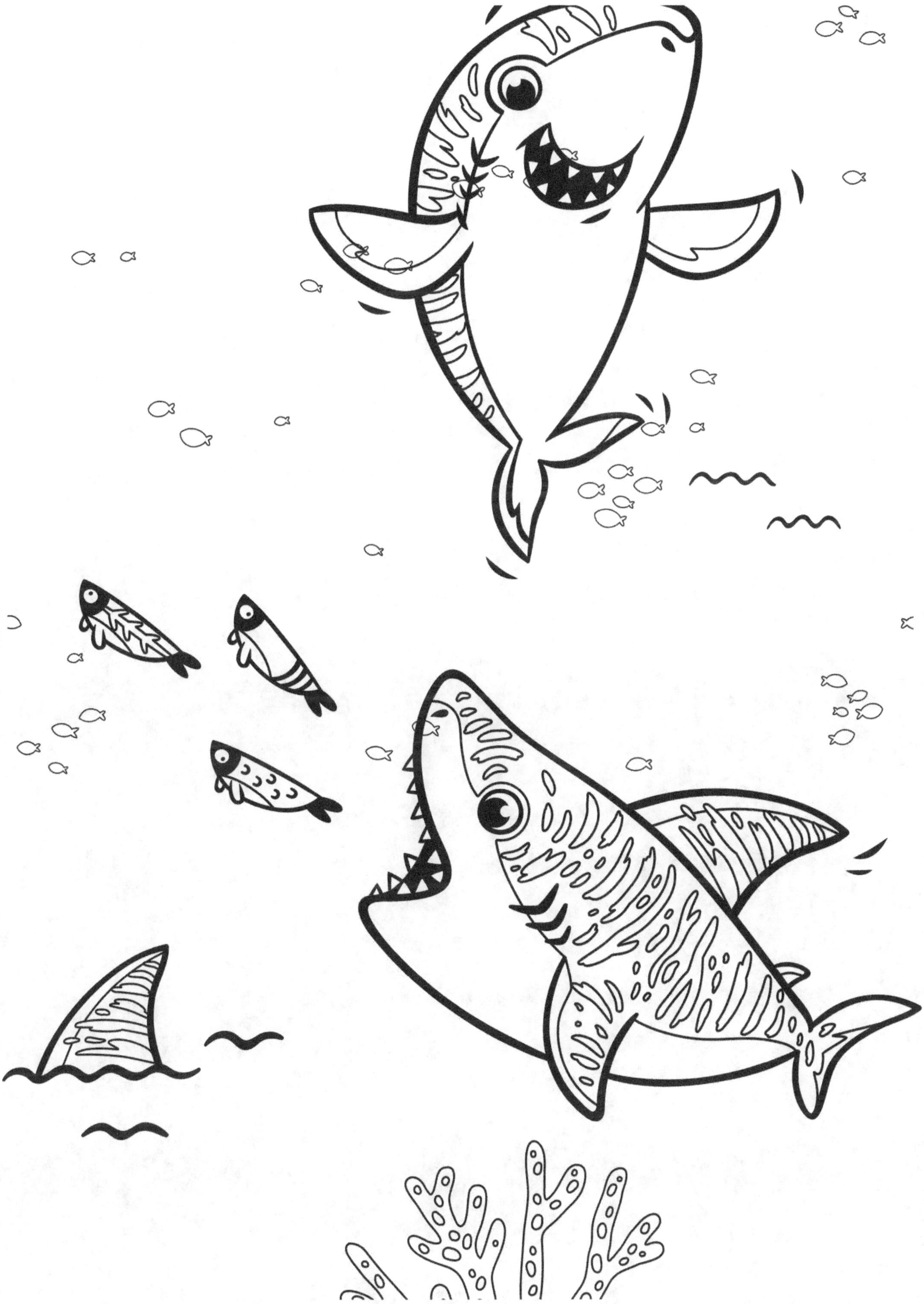

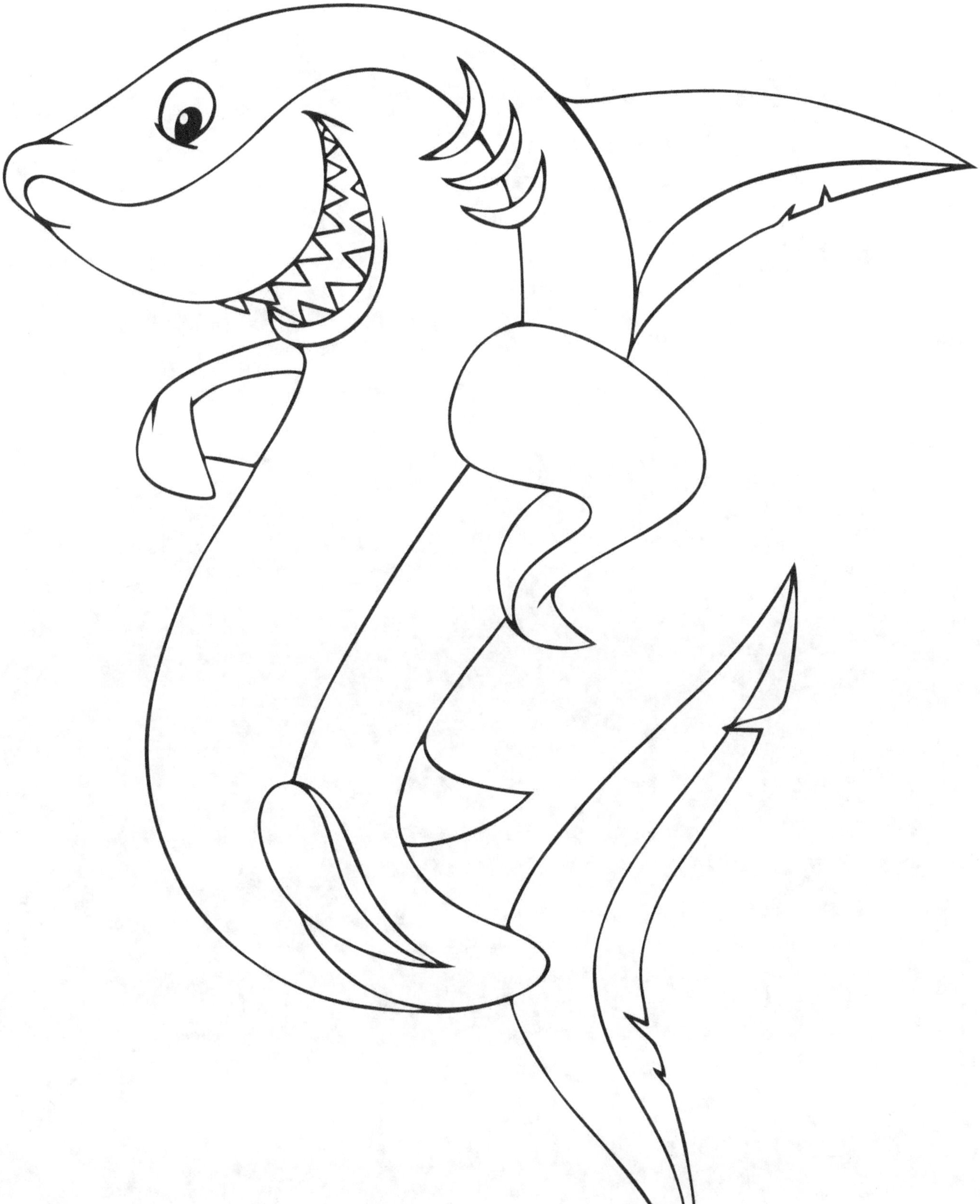

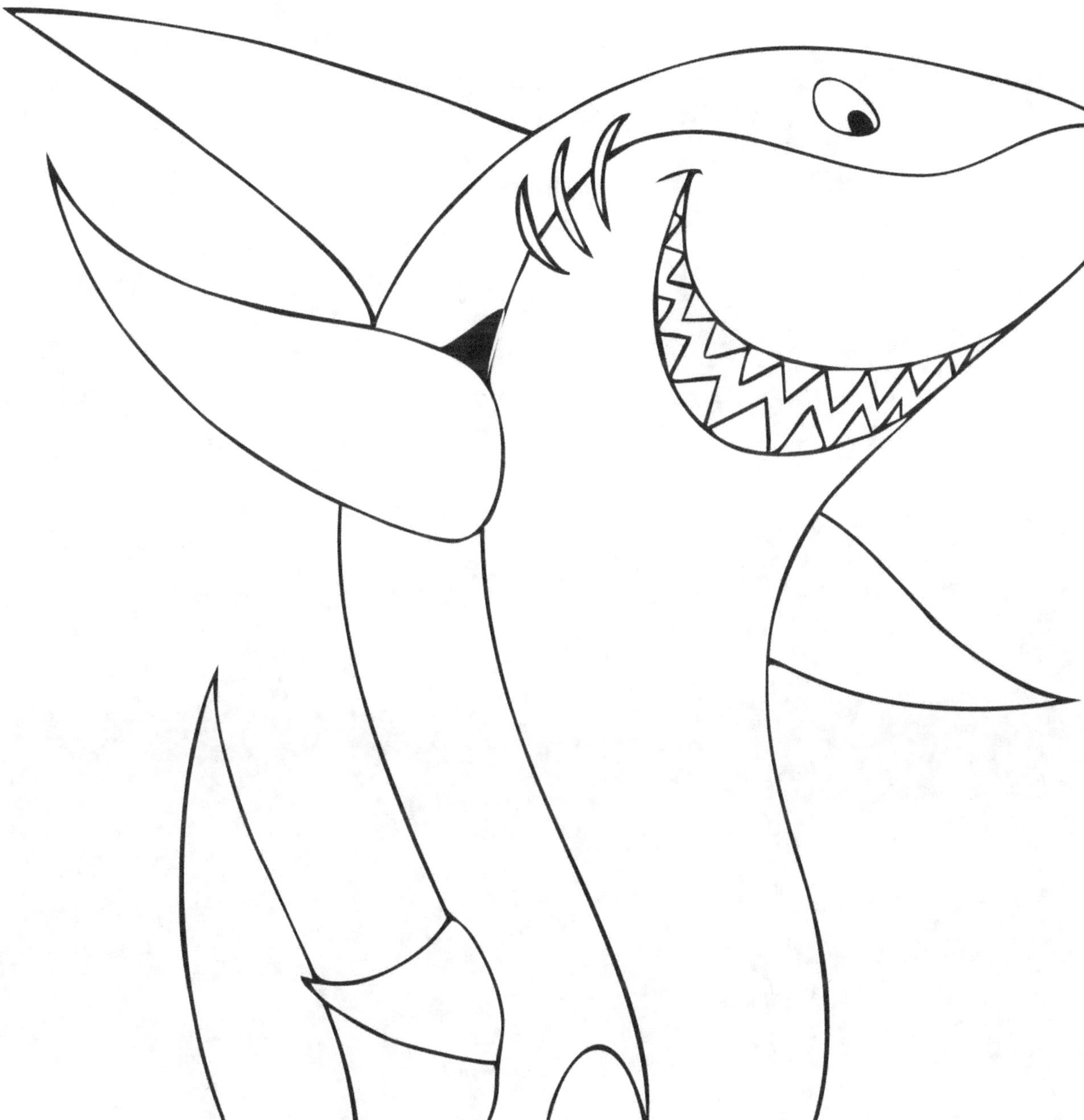

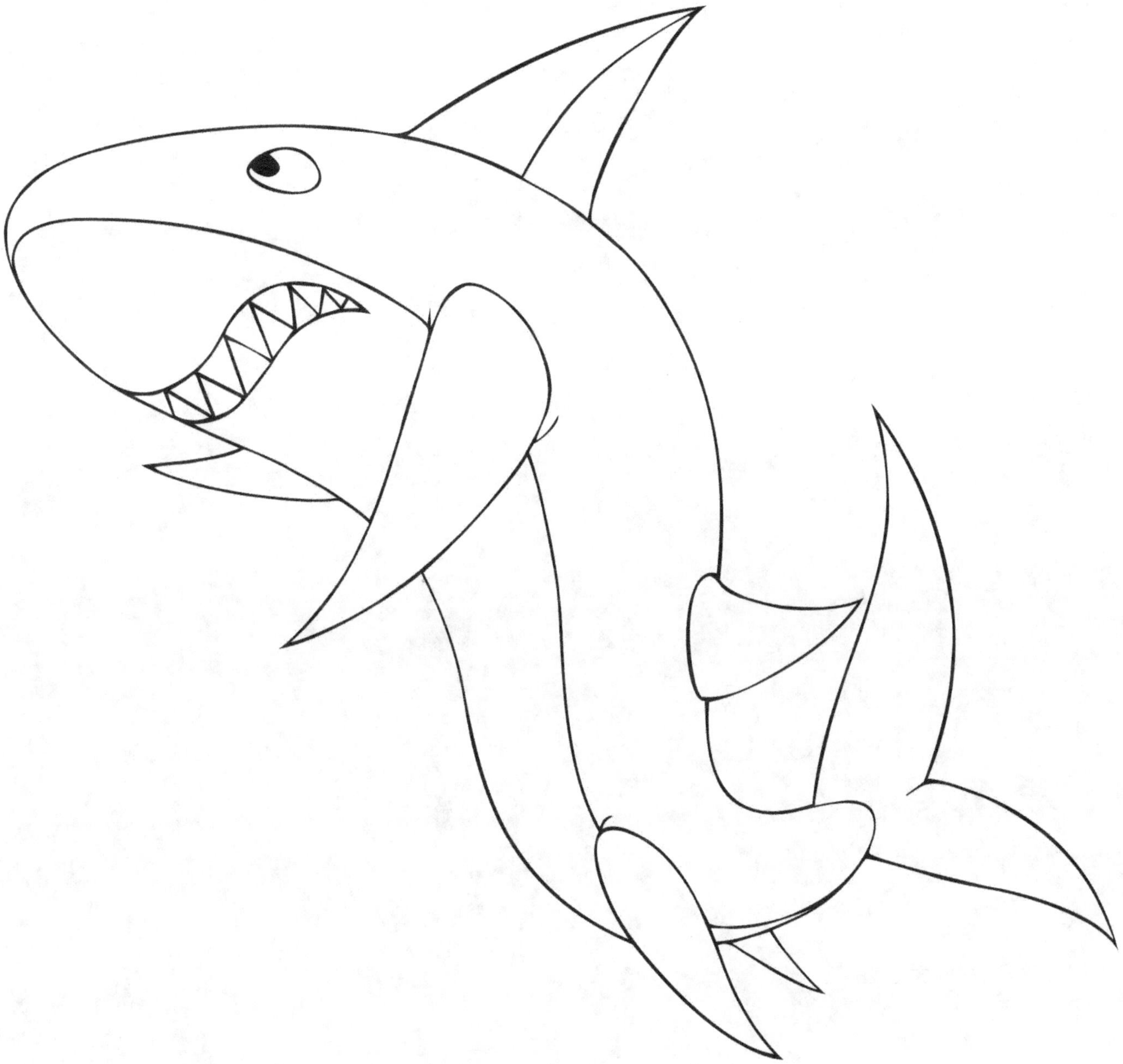

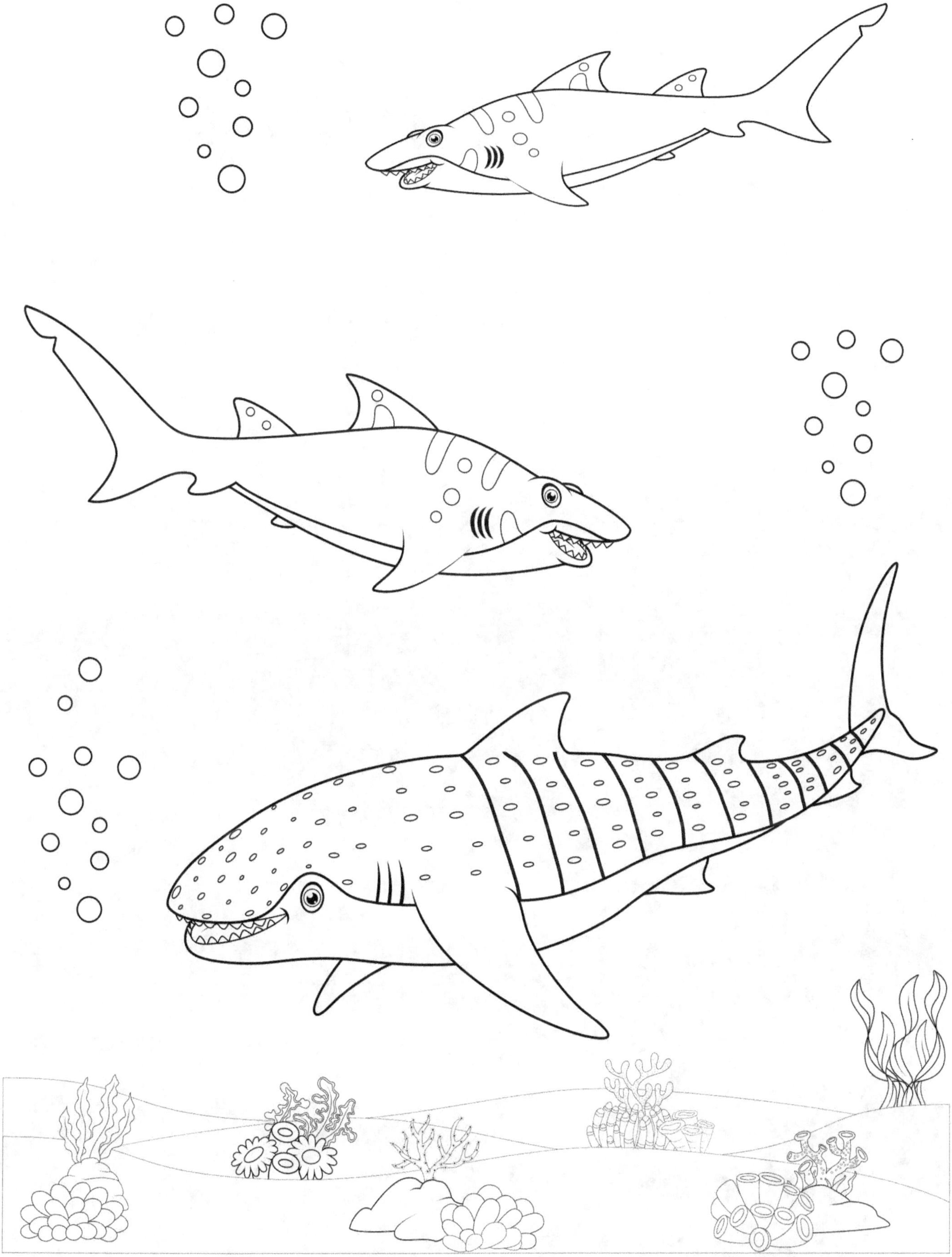

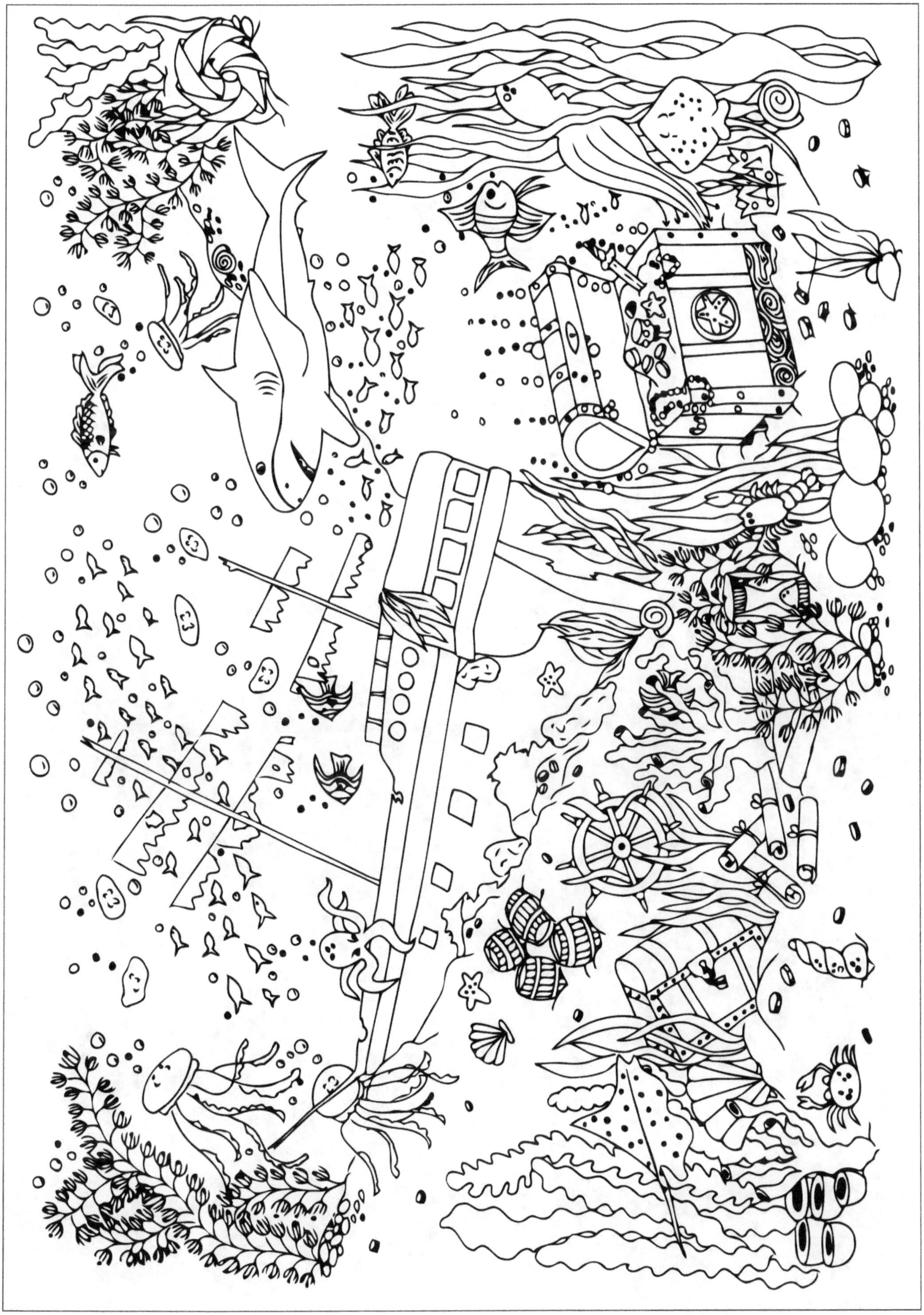

www.ingramcontent.com/pod-product-compliance
Lightning Source LLC
Chambersburg PA
CBHW081017170526
45158CB00010B/3071

* 9 7 8 1 0 7 9 9 6 0 4 2 6 *